All Screwed Up!

*Turned boxes and puzzles
featuring chased threads*

John Berkeley

Linden Publishing Inc.

2006 S. Mary

Fresno CA

To Chris, my guiding light
with love.

The author expresses his thanks to all of the following people, who have helped bring this project to fruition:

Bill Jones, for the inspiration for all of my woodturning.

Donald and Carol Goddard, without whom this book would never have been started.

Nigel, Jane and Russell at Stobart Davies for both their enthusiasm and for producing the book in such a handsome fashion.

Paul and Penny Loseby for help and support with computer matters, especially my website.

Nick Hunton of Nexus for permission to use material from *The Woodturner.*

Paul and Tracy for making me a grandad.

All Screwed Up!

All Screwed Up!
Turned Puzzles and Boxes Featuring Chased Threads

By

John Berkeley

Text and photographs by John Berkeley
Illustrations and cover design by Russell Parry

(c) 2005 Stobart Davies
135798642

ISBN: 0-941936-93-7

Printed in Singapore

A catalog record of this book is available from the Library of Congress
Library of Congress Cataloging-in-Publication Data

Berkeley, John, 1939-
All screwed up! : turned puzzles and boxes featuring chased threads / John Berkeley
p. cm.
Includes bibliographical references and index.
ISBN 0-941936-93-7 (alk. paper)
1. Turning. 2. Wooden boxes. 3. Puzzles. I. Title.
TT201.B395 2005
684".08--dc22
2004029677

Linden Publishing Inc.
2006 S. Mary
Fresno CA
www.lindenpub.com
800-345-4447

Contents

Introduction

...the story of how I became involved with woodturning, and then puzzles.

Woodturning is the most fascinating and challenging task I have so far encountered in this life. The joy of woodturning is a pleasure to be experienced. There is always the challenge, and resultant satisfaction of doing something you have never done before, and we never master everything that is possible. Occasionally there is even more satisfaction when you do something that nobody else has ever done before.

Since leaving school I have tried many things. Starting as a farm labourer I was next an Insurance agent, a salesman of day-old chicks, then of electronic components, cigars and tobacco, cigarettes, pipes, fancy goods and jewellery. In the midst of this selection I was a Police Constable for two years. I missed the company car (well, a plain one) so went back to selling. After all these exploits I ended up as a restorer of metal antiques.

During this 'antiques phase', one of my customers, a very good friend, asked if I could make a set of bone cribbage pegs for a very nice crib board he had. I have long believed that if you do not know you *cannot* do something, then you probably can... and we never *know* we cannot if we have not tried. So I said yes to his request. At the time I was the proud possessor of an old Myford ML7 metal lathe and a very small Lorch 6 mm watchmakers lathe. Neither was ideal, one being too small, the other too large. I made that very first set of crib pegs on the Lorch and was most satisfied with the result. Having really enjoyed the exercise, I was keen to repeat it. There was not a very large demand for crib pegs (though I have since made hundreds) but it occurred to me that such objects would make very attractive earrings. I duly made a set which I gave to the wife of a friend, who was a wood restorer. She was extremely pleased, but remarked how good they would look in wood.

My friend gave me a few small bits of wood for me to try, Yew and South American Tulipwood amongst them.

That was the beginning of my love affair with wood, which was easier to turn than bone and much more varied in its colours. I then enjoyed making other miniature items, but that lathe had to be upgraded. On a trip to fetch friends from Birmingham Airport one Saturday I planned to visit the Miniatura Exhibition at the NEC. Finding it to be a 'ticket only' day my dismay turned to joy when I discovered the Nexus Woodworking Show in the hall next door. I took a look inside and bought my first copy of *Woodturning* magazine (no. 23) and what at that time became my bible, Keith Rowley's *A Foundation Course for Woodturners*. I also chose my next lathe, a CARBATEC. This was upgraded to a variable speed model, and other changes followed. I now have lathes number 10 and 11, both Vicmarc VL100s which suit my every need. In the course of these changes I have made items as large as small table tops and warming pan handles, but I no longer do things of that size.

As a restorer of antique metals, with fluctuating fortunes, there was a time when I needed some capital. I had built up quite a collection of dominoes, mostly antique, and my wood restorer friend suggested I visit Camden Passage in Islington, London, where there was a shop, Donay, specializing in antique games, juvenilia and ephemera. My first visit there not only solved my initial problem, as I could see that the shop was full of dominoes, but set me thinking about other areas. Within the shop chess, backgammon, cribbage boards and much else abounded. My old selling habits came to the fore and I asked if all the crib boards had pegs. Imagine my joy when I was told by the owner, Donald Goddard, that he needed lots of sets of crib pegs, some completing and some making. In due course his wife and co-owner, Carol, sorted out a whole lot of pegs for me to make.

This went on for a year or so, after which Donald one day asked if I could repair chess pieces. I did not know I could not so my answer was, 'yes, of course!' Another year or so had gone by when he asked 'can you cut threads in wood?' I told him that, of course I could. I had read a book which gave explicit instructions. He said he would send me a picture of a puzzle and if I could make one then he thought we were onto something.

Ever since reading my first copy of *Woodturning* magazine I had become enthralled with the writings of one of the contributors, Bill Jones, so when his first 40 articles were published in book form how could I resist? It is from these, and subsequent writings, that almost everything of which I am now capable has sprung. Also, I discovered that Bill had his own connection with Donay, having turned some exquisite cannon puzzles for them. Having made contact with him myself, I am now proud to count Bill not only as my mentor, but as a friend.

With the aid of the instructions on hand chasing threads in Bill's book I made the first puzzle, a Barrel and Ball (see p13). When Donald received it he phoned immediately with his approval and sent five more pictures! These six puzzles formed the first set that eventually became one of the four sets which are marketed under the name 'Donay Hoffmann Puzzles'. These four sets of six were all taken from a book, *Puzzles Old and New*, first published in 1893 by Professor Louis Hoffmann. This book was then edited by L. E. Hordern and republished by him with lavish colour photographs of many of the original puzzles. Edward, who had the largest UK puzzle collection, and purchased many of his puzzles from the shop over the years, had given Donay a copy of the book. He also gave his blessing to the project. The copies I make are generally improved by using exotic woods, many of which were unavailable in the Victorian era, and in some cases there are other small changes.

After the first twenty-four were made (in numbers varying from a few to quite a lot) Donald suggested we try to make some puzzles of our own. He made the suggestions. I had to work out the means of operation and construction. This led to five more puzzles, all of them quite complex but using mostly principles taken from the Victorian ones. Two of them, the Apple and the Pear, were actually three puzzles in one. The Apple won a commendation in the very first International Puzzle Competition, held in Tokyo in 2001 and third prize in the Open competition at the Nexus Show in the same year.

In late 2002 Donald asked if it would be possible to miniaturize some of the puzzles. As a result I have now made 12 miniature puzzles which should hit the market in 2004. Sadly, after a short illness, Donald died in August 2003. His wife, Carol, continues with the business and is working with me to produce the existing series and develop new ideas so that the work that was Donald's brainchild may be a fitting tribute to his memory. To him I owe a great debt of gratitude for pointing my turning life in the direction which it has now taken. Without his input and encouragement I would not be writing this. Thank you Donald.

These puzzles have provided me with great pleasure over the years. I now not only make them, but also demonstrate their making. I felt it wrong to keep all the fun to myself, so a year or two ago I started writing articles on how to turn them. A number of these articles have been published in *The Woodturner* magazine (now *The Woodworker incorporating The Woodturner*) for which I am grateful. Many of the chapters of this book are re-worked versions of the articles I have written, and I am most appreciative of the generosity of the editor, Nick Hunton at Nexus, for allowing me to use the articles as a basis for this book.

Measurements

All measurements in this book are approximate and can be varied according to the wood you have available. or choose to use. Metric/Imperial conversions are therefore also approximate. What is important are the proportions of each puzzle, should you decide to vary the size.

I normally size up the male spigot, for threads, by tapering it to allow the completed female thread to leave a wax ring at the narrow end that indicates the correct size for the spigot on which to chase the male thread.

The size of thread chasers used is also a matter of choice, though I have used those I feel most appropriate for each situation. Not every one has a variety of sizes to choose from, so use the ones you have available provided they will do the job. The two most useful sizes are 20 and 24 tpi.

I would recommend that, before starting any of the puzzles, careful attention is paid to the illustrations and, where applicable, the diagrams.

The Puzzles

In 1893 Professor Louis Hoffmann published a book, entitled *Puzzles old and new*. This book is sadly not easy to obtain. I have, with the advice and help of Donald Goddard, adapted some of these puzzles and, thanks to present availability of imported hardwoods, have improved them. In some cases I have made them even more difficult to solve.

I have tried to give the basic methods and dimensions for construction of the puzzles in the instructions for the projects that follow, but both method and measurements are open to variations according to your taste and needs. The wood suggested for each puzzle can also be varied.

Most of the tools and methods I use are learned from the master, Bill Jones. The sections following this deal with tools and methods, but a read of Bill's books is a very worthwhile exercise.

Photography

For the pictures in this book I have used a Ricoh RCD7 digital camera. This is one of the few cameras with a screen that revolves 180 degrees, enabling me to see exactly what pictures I am taking. Virtually all of the illustrations are taken by myself with this camera mounted on a tripod in front of the lathe. This gives the best view, as if you were sitting in the front row at a demonstration. I use the timer so that almost all pictures are action shots. This accounts for the fact that in some of them small parts are out of focus, as the object may be moving at the time the slow shutter opens. They are all taken with normal lighting in order to avoid too many shadows.

Tools and safety

As I have already said, my inspiration comes from Bill Jones and as a result most of the tools I use are derived from his teachings.

Lathes

I have two Vicmarc VL100 variable speed lathes. These suit my every need at present, and I expect they will as long as I continue to turn. Had I the knowledge in advance that I have now, I would be able to afford three! However the experience I have gained from the other lathes I have owned has been worth the price. It puts me in a good position to advise others on the whys and wherefores of many other machines.

If you want to hand chase threads, variable speed is a great asset, though not absolutely essential. The speed of my lathes is varied by a knob, not using a foot control as Bill Jones does. I stand steadily on both feet and would most likely miss this benefit if one foot were devoted to controlling the speed. The need to change speed so often will persuade many readers to either upgrade or change their own lathes. I have, for a long time, advocated the chasing of threads at about 450 rpm, faster than some others would advise. My reason for this is simple. If you do not have a variable speed lathe then this is about as slow as you can go. At 450 rpm thread chasing is within reach of nearly all turners. My estimate is that less than half of all turners have the benefit of variable speed. My lathes also have the usual centres and faceplates, but I particularly like, and mostly use, my two Stebcentres.

With these lathes I use two Vicmarc 100 chucks, each with different jaws, an Axminster Carlton and a Burnerd three jaw, both with engineering jaws. They are all 'doctored' for safe operation by removing all sharp angles on any leading edges.

Chasing tools

My tools are kept sharp using a normal grinder, a diamond disc, a diamond wheel and a diamond credit card, all from T & J Tools, Rugby. A Hamlet grinding jig enables the correct bevel angles to be maintained with ease.

The most important tool for chasing threads is the thread chaser itself. These come in matched pairs, one for female threads and one for male. They are available from several sources. I work with Hamlet Craft Tools and so mostly use their chasers, which are of high-speed steel (HSS) and are available in 16, 18, 20, 22, and 24 teeth per inch (tpi). Because I do repairs I have chasers from 8 tpi up to 32 tpi, all of which get used occasionally. To learn thread chasing the best size to start with is around 20 tpi. This is coarse enough to be used for most things at the same time as being fine enough to make learning easy. It is easier to chase fine threads than coarse, so that, having learned on 20 tpi you can then move to the coarser threads if the need ever arises. My 8 tpi chasers enable me to make chucks to fit directly onto my lathe spindle. The other obviously useful size is 16 tpi which will fit many other lathes.

Other tools

There are two other all but essential tools that I use when chasing threads. One is a recess tool, which is shaped like a miniature Dale Nish box scraper. I use this for finishing the inside shaping of the lid, at the same time as putting in a recess at the back of the female thread to prevent the chaser hitting the back wall on each traverse. The other tool is what Bill Jones calls a 'square tool'; it has a right-angle ground at its end. I have several of these with the right-angle point ground at different angles to the handle, Theoretically it is a scraper, but it actually cuts and removes a lot of material very quickly. The purpose of these is best illustrated by the photos in the first two projects. This tool probably originates from Holtzapffel, an early nineteenth-century lathemaker (see bibliography).

In October 2003 I was lucky enough to meet Eli Avisera, a turner well known in Israel where he comes from, and also America. It was then that I first saw the range of tools he had developed and I was excited. Eli spent three days showing me some of his tricks, and the way he uses his tools.

Firstly let me briefly explain them. Eli's tools are of three distinct types. Chisels, gouges and what we describe as combination tools. Currently there are four chisels (though three more are to be added to the range): two skews, a beading tool and a parting tool. These all have, to many people's surprise, convex bevels. They need to be sharpened by an up and down movement on the grinding wheel, and then polished on a mop, either cotton or leather. This gives them that special edge which makes them a joy to use. They all have nicely rolled edges, which only contributes to their friendliness.

There are five gouges: two detail and two (with especially deeply milled flutes) bowl-cum-roughing gouges. There is also a short, $3/8$ inch (10 mm) gouge. All have very well ground back wings, giving them a fingernail profile most ladies would be proud of, and in addition a double bevel. The detail gouges do just what the name implies. The others do almost anything you want them to. They are all capable of both planing and shear-scraping cuts.

The combination tools are real hybrids. The two smaller ones are safe enough for even juveniles to use and will do almost anything a gouge will do. They are fingernail shaped and all of these tools have a small bevel, which gives them a real cutting capability. The larger ones are ideal for hollowing, and are very strong. They give an excellent finish when used in shear-scraping mode.

This range of tools are all very well finished and come with smart black ash handles. They have been greeted with admiration by several professional turners and will, I think, find an important place in the world of woodturning.

As well as these fantastic tools I have the usual armoury of gouges and skews in various sizes and with varying angles, though the Eli Avisera tools now get most use. My favourite general tool is a point tool, made famous, though not invented, by Bill Jones. I have several sizes, though I mostly use a $1/4$ inch (8 mm) or $3/8$ inch (10 mm) one. Many of the tools that I use have been home made or are modifications of existing tools. A very good example is the square tool modified from a parting tool.

I occasionally use vernier callipers and other measuring devices, but their use is limited as thread sizes can be transferred by methods described in other chapters.

The amazing armrest

Another essential is the armrest, again popularized by Bill Jones in his writings. When you first try to use an armrest you may well find it difficult. I think this is down to the way our brains work. When we hold our woodturning gouge or whatever in the usual way, we use both hands and our brain can cope. Put the tool in one hand and an armrest in the other and, like trying to pat your head and rub your tummy, the brain finds it very difficult at first. Both these exercises can be achieved with practice, so this you must do. The rewards will more than repay your persistence, and you will soon wonder how you ever managed without your armrest. It will be useful for much more than just chasing female threads.

Health and safety

Health and safety is a subject usually given insufficient thought. I think the main reason for this is the cost of implementing it in a hobby environment. Dust extractors can be improvised from old vacuum cleaners until further expense can be justified, but most people find their noise prohibitive. It is important to remove all possible traces of dust so that your lungs are maintained in a reasonable state. We can all buy an extractor, and replace it when worn out, but we do not have the same luxury when it comes to our lungs. Please breathe clean air.

My own precautions are threefold. I have an extractor nozzle right in front of my lathe, which takes a good deal of material away as it comes off the tools. I have a respirator helmet which I also use for the worst, and most dusty, woods. In addition, fixed to the ceiling, I have an Axminster CT 510D ambient air filter, which removes particles down to 1 micron. This is the quietist such filter I know of. It also has the benefit of a timer, which enables it to be left on after work to clear the invisible dust which lingers in the air.

Any chucks you use should be 'doctored' for safety, by filing or grinding all leading edges. In the event of your hand making contact you may then have only a bruise instead of a gash.

Finally, any loose clothing and hair *must* be kept well out of the way at all times in the workshop.

Choice of Woods

This chapter contains information on the woods which I have found suitable for the hand chasing of threads. It cannot be a full list, as there are undoubtedly suitable woods which I have not tried. The information on, and Latin names of, each wood I have gleaned from a number of sources, and to the best of my knowledge is correct.

The woods which are best for thread chasing are close-grained hardwoods, mostly imported, and generally at the more expensive end of the market. My three favourites are Boxwood, African Blackwood and Mopane, giving a fair spectrum of colour ranging from light straw, through red/brown to very black, though Blackwood varies considerably, with a most attractive grain pattern. These three woods enable the cutting of very crisp threads. I also use most varieties of Rosewood, including Santos (not strictly a Rosewood) South American Tulipwood, Kingwood (both true Rosewoods) Pink Ivory, Satine Bloodwood, Cocobolo, Piquia Amarello, Lignum Vitae, Snakewood, and the heartwood of Yew, and a few others. It is, however, possible to cut threads in many other woods with the aid of cyanoacrylate or epoxy resin. I have covered this process in the section on thread chasing (p 9).

Most of these woods produce toxic dust when turned. The two most notorious are Cocobolo and Santos Rosewood. It is common sense, when turning, to employ every means possible to protect oneself not only from the dangers of this and any wood dust, but also any thing that might hurl itself at you from the lathe. The three means to achieve this are the use of a respirator helmet, a dust extractor or vacuum cleaner placed just behind your working area, and an ambient air filter (see section on tools, p 5.)

There follows a list of suitable woods with a little more detail on each. It is important to know how dry these woods are, so I include specific gravity (SG) figures to enable those of you who have (like me) a non-invasive moisture meter to check moisture content easily. Many woods which are sold 'part-seasoned' are actually almost dripping. This is, of course, because all sources of dry timber have been exhausted and time does not permit proper drying. Care must be taken with these woods to allow them to dry,

either naturally or by artificial means. I have successfully dried part-turned Pink Ivory wood in a microwave.

BOXWOOD
Buxus sempervirens SG 0.9

A native European tree which normally does not grow to a great size. Because it is slow growing it is very close grained and a delight to all who use it. It is quite freely available in smaller sizes. Its rich honey colour gives it appeal. Box is not easy to dry without shakes and it is very prone to a grey staining, which discourages many American buyers, however this staining can lead to some very attractive colour variation.

YEW
Taxus baccata SG 0.7

A beautiful native British wood, with very attractive contrasting heartwood and sapwood. The heartwood is fine for chasing treads. Box has much superstition attached to it. The whole tree is poisonous, so take care. The wood has a tendency to split and suffers from heat shakes. With care it polishes extremely well. Many more details can be found on http://www.whitedragon.org.uk/articles/yew.htm

AFRICAN BLACKWOOD
Dalbergia melanoxylon SG 1.2

This member of the rosewood family is highly prized by turners and musical instrument makers, who demand the highest quality and will pay high prices. It is very hard and close-grained. It finishes extremely well and cuts excellent threads. I use it for all three cannons, Apple, Pear and the New, New Castle Money Box.

MOPANE
Colophospermum mopane SG 1.2

This tree, native to tropical Southern Africa, is red-brown, with most attractive grain. It turns extremely well and is used by ornamental turners and by the musical instrument trade, so it cuts excellent threads and finishes really well.

SATINE BLOODWOOD
Brosimum paraense SG 1.2
A beautiful dense, deep red wood, from Brazil, which turns well and accepts a fine finish. It is tough on tools and sensitive to heat shakes, so care is needed with sanding.

BRAZILIAN TULIPWOOD
Dalbergia frutescens SG 1.0
An attractive red-striped wood, which turns well and takes a good finish. It has a distinctive smell when being worked. Must be well dried.

KINGWOOD
Dalbergia cearensis SG 1.2
This small tree, from Brazil, rarely produces wood larger than 2" (50 mm) thick. It is most attractively striped brown-violet in colour and much sought after, hence quite expensive.

PIQUIA AMARELLO
Aspidosperma species SG 0.8
Again from Brazil, this yellow, fairly straight-grained wood is fine for threads. It is not normally found in large sizes as it cracks a lot when drying and is prone to heat shakes if not treated carefully. I have sometimes used it in place of boxwood as its colour is more consistent.

COCOBOLO
Dalbergia retusa SG 1.1
This one is from Mexico and is one of the most attractive woods. It is coloured from bright orange to red and has stripes throughout, varying in colour from light orange to almost black. It has an almost greasy surface, needing hardly any polish. Like brightly coloured insects, however, it has a sting in its tail. It produces very toxic dust and seems to affect more turners than almost any other timber, producing irritating rashes and hay fever-like symptoms. **Be careful with this wood.** Take every possible precaution, and then enjoy the results.

SANTOS ROSEWOOD
Machaerium scleroxylon SG 0.9
Also from South America, Bolivia this time, this is not a true Rosewood, though in many ways better than most Rosewoods. **This is another wood to treat with care.** It is a most attractive timber with various colours of striped grain running through it. It would be a pleasure to turn, were it not for its inherent dangers.

RED LANCEWOOD
Archidendropsis basaltica SG 1.1
This wood hails from Australia. It is locally known as 'dead finish'. A beautiful, red, figured wood which usually includes some light-coloured sapwood, showing a fine contrast. It is not easy to obtain currently, but a joy to turn. Liable to heat shakes if finished without great care.

LEADWOOD
Combretum imberbe SG 1.3
This heavier-than-water African wood is protected, so only dead or fallen trees are used. Heartwood is very dark. It tends to blunt tools, and is so hard that, before metal was available, it was used in Africa to make implements, such as hoes. It turns well and sustains a fine finish.

LIGNUM VITAE
Guaiacum officinale SG 1.25
A native to the Antilles, but now grown all over the Caribbean, Central and South America. It is so hard and so resinous that it has many engineering uses. It does not float and is self-lubricating. Locally known as Gaiac its bark was used to cure syphilis and its resin to relieve arthritis. It is resistant to most acids and other harmful chemicals and is absolutely foodsafe. Many antique wassail bowls and drinking vessels are made of Lignum.

MGURURE
Combretum schumannii SG 1.1
A rich, dark, hard wood from Africa, sometimes used as an alternative to African Blackwood. Turns well and takes a fine finish. I use this for the New Jubilee Puzzle.

MUHUHU
Brachylaena hutchinsii SG 0.9
This wood is from Tanzania; it is hard and dense with a dark yellowish brown heartwood. It exudes a pleasant spicy odour when worked and takes a good finish. It has proved successful for the Magic Mushroom variant of the Zulu Box.

SHE-OAK
Allocosuarina species SG 0.7
One of some 40 different species, most of which have a few small leaves. It is not related to Oak (*Quercus* species), but has very prominent medullary rays which give it a similar appearance. Very easy to turn and takes a very good finish.

SNAKEWOOD
Piratinera (*Brosimum*) *guianensis* SG 1.3
A very hard, reddish-brown wood, with figuring that makes it look like snakeskin. It splits very easily, and also, due to its premium price, is normally only available in small sizes. It turns very well, cuts good threads, and takes a fine finish.

PINK IVORY WOOD
Berchemia zeyheri SG 1.0
A fine, hard turning wood from Southern Africa. Mystical properties are attached to it by Zulus. Its colour varies from very light pink to red. It has a tendency to split when drying and is easily affected by heat shakes when finishing.

PAPUA NEW GUINEA (PNG) EBONY
Diospyros ferrea (or *insularis*) SG 1.0
This wood from Papua New Guinea, though it does grow elsewhere, is black with most attractive lighter stripes. It is protected and not exportable in log form. PNG ebony works well with a distinctive odour and takes a fine finish.

MALLEE BURR
Eucalyptus species SG 1.1
This Australian wood is a joy to turn, and was recently introduced to me by Simon Hope. It comes in large burrs, which for my purposes need to be sectioned into squares. It is hard, but with sharp tools turns extremely well and takes a fine finish. It is very good for thread chasing.

Thread Chasing
the whys and hows of hand chasing wooden threads

Thread chasing by hand has been practised for a very long time by hardwood turners and bone grubbers in the execution of their normal daily business. In the days before modern adhesives there was no better way to join small parts together than with threads. Some chess kings were made of up to 12 parts that screw together. Today chasing threads by hand is something of a rarity, but many woodturners are once again showing an interest in it. The benefits of threads are not hard to understand. Boxes with screw lids are much more secure and, I believe, less prone to the vagaries of climatic variation. This book illustrates over twenty puzzles, mostly with threads. If this is not reason enough to learn thread chasing, it also offers another and different challenge to turners who have done almost everything else.

Alan Batty has made an excellent demonstration video and Bill Jones, the master of thread chasing, has written extensively on the subject. It is from his writings and teaching that I learned, and so the contents of this chapter are my interpretation of his methods. If you stick to the principles that I will outline, and practise them, I am sure that you will be successful in acquiring this skill. I myself learned from a book, so it can not be too difficult. To want to chase threads you need some form of an incentive. Mine was originally that I would earn money by so doing. Threaded boxes in an infinite variety of sizes, shapes and woods are a good starting point. The variety of puzzles which I make (in excess of thirty) should be further incentive for a lot more turners to want to learn.

When you realize, in addition, the variety of puzzles that you can make it casts a whole new light on thread chasing. I feel sure that the original object of these puzzles was for turners to make them, rather than for people to solve them afterwards! To make fittings that can be screwed directly onto the headstock of your lathe is just another big advantage. A whole new range of possibilities opens up once you have mastered the skill of thread chasing.

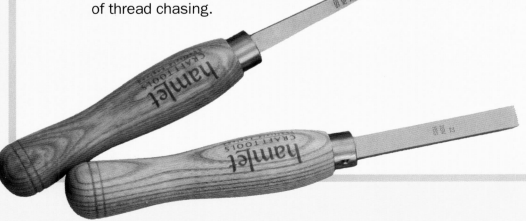

Starting thread chasing

Before you start you obviously need thread chasers, and an armrest too. Working as I do with Hamlet tools I can only endorse the quality of their high-speed steel chasers. I also use extensively their range of Ian Wilkie tools, which particularly suit the type of work I produce. For learning thread chasing the most useful size of chaser is around a 20 tpi; a size either side is acceptable. These sizes are fine enough to make learning relatively easy and coarse enough for most general threads. Other sizes can be acquired as and when the need arises, if it ever does. When you buy many new chasers they need rendering user-friendly, by rounding off all sharp edges and smoothing down the back surface, so that when moving along the tool rest (similarly smoothed) travel is free and easy. Hamlet do this to all their chasers before they leave the factory.

Virtually any wood can be used, though hard woods cut the best threads. By and large, if the wood is expensive it is probably good for chasing threads. This need not prevent most woodturners from trying. Softer woods, such as native fruit woods, can be rendered hard with several applications of cyanoacrylate adhesive, as recommended by Bonnie Klein. Coat the spigot with Superglue and, when dry, begin to chase a thread. When you start to cut through the glue layer, stop and give it another coat. Repeat the process several times until the thread is finished and your thread will be as good as one cut in the hardest of wood. It takes a little longer but if time is not money then what the heck! One word of warning; rub candle wax into the teeth of your chaser to prevent it clogging with glue.

Another alternative was shown to me by its originator, Petter Herud, from Norway. His home country has a wide range of most attractive native woods which are virtually all, sadly, too soft to take a normal thread. His method is to cut a channel where the thread needs to go and fill it with either plain or coloured epoxy resin. When cured (set) this allows perfect threads to be chased, so enabling these woods to be used for screw-threaded boxes.

A lot of the wood I have used is sold, like a vast amount of imported hardwood, 'part-seasoned'. This is a very good euphemism for 'pretty wet'. I have successfully dried it in a microwave cooker, after rough turning to shape and hollowing, leaving the walls about 10 mm thick.

If you decide to do this **take these important precautions:**

1 Use only on the lowest setting and give a number of 'cooks' at spaced intervals. By regular, accurate weighing it is possible to see when the blanks have stopped losing weight and are therefore dry. I usually dry wood in this way over a weekend, leaving about two hours between each period of cooking.

2 Make certain your partner is not in the kitchen!

The woods that I have found best, and which I use regularly, for thread chasing are African Blackwood and Boxwood, but I also use extensively Mopane, Pink Ivory, Kingwood, Tulipwood, Santos Rosewood, Amazon Rosewood, Yew heartwood, Cocobolo, Mgrure, Mhuhu, Snakewood, Red Lancewood, She-oak and Leadwood. Providing you stick to the darker heartwood of Yew this is probably the least expensive English wood to practise on, and if you are to succeed in thread chasing practise must be your watchword.

It is best to practise first on a long male spigot, though it is easier for the purpose of sizing to cut the female thread first when making boxes.

The principle is simple. The chaser needs to move along the spigot, then be withdrawn and moved back ready to start again. The easiest way to achieve this is to practise a circular, anticlockwise motion of the chaser on the tool rest with a regular, even rhythm before you touch the wood. If you reverse the motion of travel you end up with a left-hand thread. Which is about as sinister as it gets.

10

1 Cut a spigot, for practice not too short, chamfer the end and cut a groove at the shoulder end to prevent the chaser hitting the back wall on each traverse.

2 Thread chasing is a scraping, rather than cutting, action so set the tool rest a little above centre and about 12 mm (a fingers-width) away from the spigot, ensuring the chaser is trailing. Make certain the tool rest is absolutely smooth and allows the chaser to move freely. Have the left-hand end of the tool rest about level with the shoulder of the spigot. This makes the 'Bill Jones' grip easy, with fingers beneath and thumb on top of the chaser, giving you the ultimate delicate control.

3 Start the lathe on the lowest speed you can, which is about 400–450 rpm on most lathes.

4 Cut a recess at the back end of the spigot to enable time and space for the chaser to be removed on each pass, before hitting the shoulder.

5 Practise the regular circular motion (described on p 10) a few times before very gently touching the chamfer with the **centre** teeth of the thread chaser. On no account try to start with the first tooth of the chaser. The technique works easily if the chaser is at an angle of about 45% to the lathe axis.

6 Just a few gentle touches, using the regular rhythm you have already established, starts the thread. This then enables slight pressure to be applied towards the centre-line, on each subsequent pass, and for the thread to be continued up to the shoulder, by moving your right hand gradually to your left. The operative word in all this is **gentle**. Any effort to control the tool usually results in a good series of rings rather than a thread. Thread chasing is not like the turning most people are used to, where the tool needs to be gripped with both hands and 'shown where to go'.

And for a female thread?

That is the essence of thread chasing. For the female thread you need a hole, not a spigot, with a similar run off for the chaser, and the motion is clockwise. When practising it is far easier to start with a hole all the way through your blank. A chamfer on the front edge (as with the male thread) is also necessary. Another great help is an armrest; I use the Bill Jones style once again. The armrest most people find a bit cumbersome to start with, but regular use soon renders it an indispensable part of your turning armoury. Mine is kept on a leather thong around my neck and is with me, ready to be used, all the time I am turning. In use it is held under the left arm and at right-angles to, and resting on, the tool rest. The tool is held on it by the left thumb and the whole armrest is moved with the chaser on it. For the female thread use the reverse motion to that employed for the male thread. Use of the armrest goes much further than just for thread chasing, as those who have seen me demonstrate will testify. It is used for hollowing and drilling and lends itself to considerable accuracy for both these operations.

Reducing the diameter

If either thread needs reducing in size do so with the tool of your choice, but not the chaser. Using the chaser for this purpose usually results in a crumbled thread. Too great or variable a speed of traverse often results in a double-start thread.

Size matching

Practise the male thread to begin with, though when making boxes it is easier to finish the female thread first. For an accurate size match between corresponding threads, cut a tapered spigot which, when touched by the finished, waxed female thread, acquires a wax ring on its tapered end. I find the easiest way to transfer the mark is to hold the waxed female end against the spigot for the male thread as it revolves in the chuck. The mark so created indicates the diameter for the spigot on which to chase the male thread. When using expensive hardwoods, and those with a really fancy grain which you want to retain, this method of matching wastes less of the grain pattern. To retain continuity of grain pattern it is necessary to remove wood, a small amount at a time, from the rear wall of the spigot.

Practice, practice, practice!

Bill Jones suggests that when you have made 50 boxes you will have an idea of how thread chasing is done. I recommend that every time you go to your lathe you chase at least one thread. Do this every day for a month or two and you will know how to chase threads in wood. What satisfaction this will then give you.

For a more comprehensive set of pictures, and to avoid duplication, look at the pictures in Basic Boxes and the subsequent projects.

Box Basics

Boxes can be made in a great variety of shapes, sizes and woods, offering tremendous scope for personal style. Box making is the first step to making most of the puzzles which follow in this book, so this chapter is intended as an introduction to the kind of skills you will need to develop.

When making any box, as with most turning, it is important to get the balance right. The golden rule should be applied so that one dimension, such as height, is about one and a half times the other dimension, the diameter, and the lid is made from about a third of the height of the blank. The illustrations here show this and also give an idea of some other interesting shapes.

What follows on the next three pages is my usual sequence of tasks for making a simple box.

1

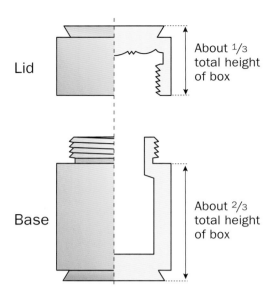

Lid — About 1/3 total height of box

Base — About 2/3 total height of box

Part off from your cylinder the third at the chuck end to make the lid. Remember to allow length in the lower two thirds for a spigot, for holding the box for hollowing and to finish the lid, as well as a spigot for the male thread.

2

Hollow out the lid and finish the inside surface; I usually use the same sort of pattern.

Now chase a thread of your choice.

Remember to make a run off, or recess, so that your chaser does not hit the bottom of the lid on each traverse. The smaller the box, the finer the thread. Most boxes work best with 16 tpi, 18 tpi or 20 tpi, but try chasing first with 20 tpi chasers.

Wax the thread ready to mark the male spigot (see step **3**); clean any excess wax out of the thread with a toothbrush.

3

Remount the bottom section and cut a slightly oversize spigot.

Having held the waxed, female thread against the revolving spigot to mark it, reduce the taper to the size indicated by the wax mark. Now chase a thread on which to screw the lid, leaving a run off, or recess, at the back of the thread, as with the lid.

4

Screw on your lid to allow the outside to be shaped.

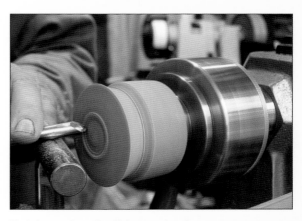

Finish turning the lid completely.

5

Then turn the outside of the base to the shape you have chosen. This is best done with the lid still in place, so you have an idea of the overall balance.

Now the lid can be polished.

6

Hollow the bottom in the manner most appropriate to the box's final shape and finish.

Wax the thread so a male spigot can be marked.

7

Now make a screw chuck on which to remount the bottom, so that its base can be turned clean and finished.

Remember to leave a small foot on which the base can stand if the bottom is rounded.

8

The bottom and top spigots can often be used as part of the design of the box. Possibilities are limitless, and designs can be introduced to suit your ability, flights of fancy and the piece of wood at hand.

In the Soup

The object of In the Soup is to remove the ball using the 'spoon' without tipping the bowl.

This puzzle is exasperatingly difficult to solve without some clue as to its solution. It is an ideal introduction to the intriguing world of turned puzzles for those who are not yet at the stage of hand chasing threads.

The size shown here is about right if you use common marbles, but what good practice for turning spheres, if you want to make them larger! In the Soup is a simple bowl, turned in Goncalo Alves, 89 mm (3 1/2") in diameter and 76 mm (3") deep.

The spoon handle is Blackwood, the working end a length of brass brazing rod, flattened and slightly bent at the end.

Of this puzzle Professor Hoffmann says:

> *'It demands a steady hand and a considerable amount of patience, the ball having a provoking way of escaping from the spoon and falling 'in the soup' again just at the very moment when the neophyte thinks he has at last succeeded.'*

The puzzle itself is simplicity to make, being just a small bowl. Nor should the spoon present any difficulty. I use brass, as in the original, but I have seen one made in wood with the end hand carved, which should be just as effective.

89mm (3½")

76mm (3")

1

The Goncalo Alves blank ready to be shaped.

2

Rough turning the outside of the bowl.

3

Turning the outside to the basic shape.

4

Final shaping of the outside.

5

Hollowing the inside to the correct depth; taking out a central core.

6

Turning the inside of the bowl.

7

Shear scraping the inner surface.

8

Sanding the inside and top part of outside, down to 1200 grit.

9

Following the 1200 grit by polishing.

10

Reverse-chucked on a shaped spigot and protected with paper, the lower part of the outside can now be shaped.

11

Flattening and slightly bending the end of the brass spoon. This will now need to be sanded and polished.

12

Finding the centre of the handle prior to drilling to take the brass rod.

13

Drilling the hole to receive the brass rod.

14

Shaping the African Blackwood handle.

Shape the spoon end to look something like this.

SOLUTION

This puzzle is a real teaser. I have only seen one person solve it legitimately. There is no 'trick'; you just need a steady hand. The degree of difficulty posed by any particular puzzle depends, of course, on the exact shape of the spoon, and the size of the ball.

Tire 'em Out

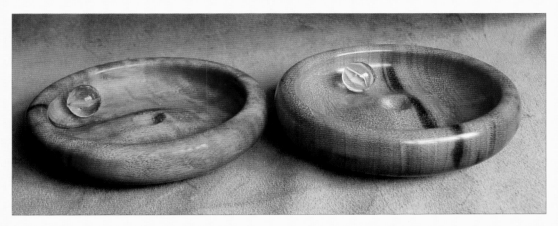

The object of this puzzle is to get the ball into the centre — without touching the ball.

This puzzle itself is simple to make, many turners have remarked that their bowls normally finish up looking like this one! But it is not so simple to solve. Quite simply it is a shallow bowl with a gradually inclined bottom and a small dimple in the centre. I try to make it an object of beauty with the underside finished as attractively as the inside. They can be made in any wood you have available. I have turned ones in Cherry, Goncalo Alves, Padauk, Yew and Ash over the years. The original Victorian puzzles, from which this one is derived, were made of tin and painted. I think wood is much better. The original seems to have been made in France.

On a box lid of one such original is:

GAME OF EQUILIBRIUM, or the INTELLECT-OM-ETER.

A massive intellect will get the marble into the hole ten times in a minute.

A moderate intellect five times in a minute.

A poor intellect once in a minute.

A very inferior intellect once in two or more minutes.

A wretched intellect may not get it in at all, and may be long trying becoming a howling lunatic.

DIRECTIONS [which are in five languages]
You must cause the marble to arrive in the hole by means of the movement of the plate.

The following illustrations shows how I make them. I normally make them in pairs, as this utilizes the wood more efficiently.

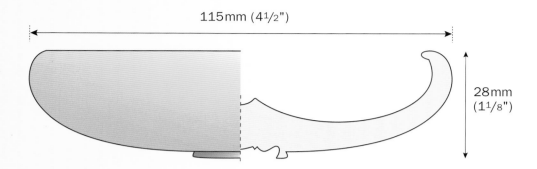

115mm (4¹/₂")

28mm
(1¹/₈")

1

A bowl blank, 115mm (4¹/₂") in diameter and 60mm (2³/₈") deep is held between centres to allow the formation of a recess on its base to enable it to be held in the chuck. The outline is a little blurred because the blank is not exactly centred, but it will be trued up later.

2

Held in expansion mode on a chuck; the parting point is evident. Roughly turn the base of one half to shape.

3

Turn the outside of the bowl to its final shape now.

4

Sand the base down to 1200 grit, for a fine finish.

5

Polish the base.

6

With the blank reversed in the chuck, the second base can be turned to shape...

7

... and polished.

8

Having been parted, the two insides (one at a time, obviously!) can now be hollowed.

9

And hollowed some more.

10

Sand, as with the outside, down to 1200 grit.

11

Finally polish the inside of the bowl.

12 Repeat steps 8–11 for the second bowl and you have a lovely pair of puzzles with which to tease your friends.

Though I use marbles, there is no reason why you should not make your own spheres in some exotic contrasting hardwood.

SOLUTION

The only method I know to succeed with this little devil is to tilt the bowl very slightly towards you, holding it with only one hand. Once the marble is still, move the bowl sharply towards you so that the marble, remaining stationary by inertia, drops into the hole. Even this may take a little practice. The original book comments that:

'This method is, however, scarcely legitimate. The marble should be rolled, not jerked, into position.'

Barrel and Ball

The object is to remove the ball without smashing the barrel!

The first puzzle that Donald Goddard asked me to try to make for him was the Barrel and Ball. Its construction is very simple, once you have mastered the art of hand thread chasing. It is, in essence, just a box, with the barrel forming the 'lid'. Simplicity is its appeal. The barrel contains a ball, which can be heard on shaking the puzzle, but no obvious means of exit is apparent. The Blackwood peg is essential to its correct solution. The original (and my earlier attempts) had a peg which could be completely removed. This helped add to the intrigue, but usually led to the peg being lost, so I now make them with the peg held captive by a small, internal, hand-made screw.

The wood I normally use for this puzzle is Pink Ivory, though it also looks splendid in Mopane and many other woods. The originals were almost exclusively made in Box, but this lacks the visual appeal of the woods I have mentioned.

Not only can the Barrel and Ball be made in different woods, but also in sizes ranging from about 15mm upwards, though for the smaller sizes small fingers are needed. This means that, as with all of these puzzles, any dimensions are arbitrary and can be varied to suit your available wood and thread-chasing tools.

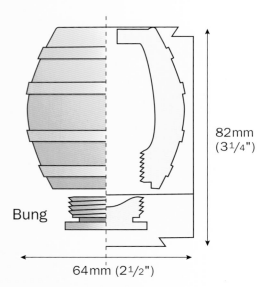

82mm (3¹/₄")

64mm (2¹/₂")

Bung

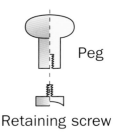

Peg

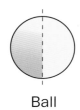

Retaining screw

Ball

1

Turn a cylinder, about 64 mm (2¹/₂") in diameter and 82 mm (3¹/₄") long, with a spigot at each end.   This is a useful practice enabling the blank to be held, when needed, by its opposite end. So long as these spigots are not too small in diameter then almost no wood will be lost.

2

Part off 64 mm (2¹/₂") from the holding spigot. The remaining 19 mm (³/₄") will later form the bung .

3

Hollow to a depth of 51 mm (2"), as in the diagram. The internal wall can be shaped, if you like, to allow the ball to rattle better when the barrel is shaken. Carefully chase a 16 tpi female thread and wax. This is important to allow measurement for the male thread (see **6**).

4

Cut a 6 mm (¹/₄") recess at the extreme end to allow the bung to seat without the thread showing.

5

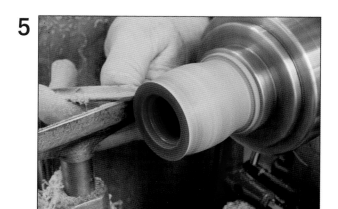

Turn to a rough barrel shape. This will be refined later when it is mounted from the opposite end, screwed onto the bung which then acts as a chuck.

6

Remount the other 19 mm (^{3}/$_4$") long part of the blank (the bung), and turn a tapered spigot, such that the waxed female thread leaves a ring on its outer end, denoting the correct diameter for the thread to be cut.

7

Cut a crisp thread to fit into the barrel. This must be free to unscrew easily, or the puzzle may jam at a later date, as this neophyte puzzle-maker found to his cost.

8

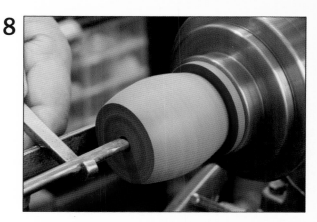

Screw on the previously made barrel and drill a hole, about 7.5 mm (^{5}/$_{16}$") in diameter, to take the peg, which must be made a loose fit.

9

Now carefully shape the barrel section, with its bands, and mark a part-off point on the bung for the base of puzzle. This will leave a lip of about 4 mm (^{1}/$_8$") which, when screwed up will conceal the existence of the bung.

10

Barrel is now ready for polishing.

11

Part-off the bung.

12

Fix a piece of scrap wood in the chuck, hollow it and chase a thread in the hollow to enable the bung to be screwed into it.

13

Now finish its flat surface so that it seats a little below the base rim.

14

Start turning a ball from a 25 mm (1") diameter Blackwood blank.

15

Turn the ball so that it fits loosely inside the barrel. This enables it to rattle well.

16

With the remainder of the Blackwood blank drill a hole and tap it with a $^3/_{16}$" Whitworth thread.

17

Now turn about 19 mm ($^3/4$") of its length to the 7.5 mm ($^3/16$") diameter of the hole in the barrel, so that it fits loosely. Add a knob to the top end, part-off and finish. It is best to tap the thread before this shaping, so there is less chance of the wood splitting.

18

The last task before assembly is to make the retaining screw, which, when screwed into the end of the peg inside the barrel, keeps it there and prevents the peg from being lost. The head must be larger than the top hole of the barrel and should be made concave so that when pressed against the ball, there is maximum surface area contact.

19

Chase a 24 tpi thread on the retaining screw.

All the components of the Barrel and Ball puzzle.

SOLUTION

Grasp the barrel in your left hand, with forefinger on base and thumb on top of the peg, squeezing together, to enable the body to be unscrewed. This classic puzzle, when carefully made will give you hours of fun trying it out on your unsuspecting friends. The original idea came from a book published in 1893 by Professor Louis Hoffmann.

The Zulu Box

This puzzle is a sort of Victorian pill box; the objective is to remove the lid.

The Zulu Box is a real favourite of mine, as it uses such a simple principle, yet so baffles most people. Following Stuart King's suggestion it becomes even more perplexing with the addition of a coin inside, which acts very successfully as a 'red herring'.

I normally make this puzzle in Satine Bloodwood, a most attractive, dark red, South American hardwood, though as with all these puzzles it can be made in any wood suitable for thread chasing. The shape I normally make is based on illustrations in an 1893 book by Professor Louis Hoffmann. The idea has been adapted by David Springett, in his book *Woodturning Trickery*, to a mushroom shape (see below), which I also sometimes make. Dimensions can be altered to suit your own wood supplies. I have made the Zulu Box in sizes from as little as 16 mm ($^5/8$") high, to the size shown here. For pills about 32 mm ($1^1/4$") is most suitable.

Construction of the Zulu Box is hardly more difficult than for a simple, screw-lidded box, but you need to master thread chasing first. Originally I made these boxes with 16 tpi threads, but around 20 tpi is easier to master, and will do the job just as well. It is essential to make the thread operate perfectly, for reasons which will become clear later in step **6**.

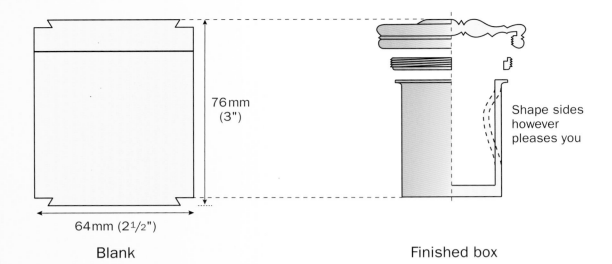

76mm
(3")

64mm (2½")

Blank

Shape sides
however
pleases you

Finished box

1

Turn a blank 64mm (2½") diameter and 76mm (3") long, with spigots at both ends. The spigot at the lid end will later be used to form part of the raised pattern on its top surface.

2

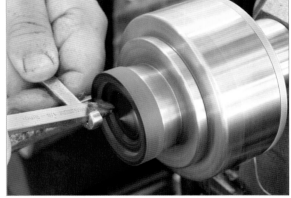

Part off the lid about 19mm (³/4") from the chuck to allow you to hollow and chase a 16tpi thread as in the diagram.

3

Finish the inside of the lid with a pattern, *à la* Bill Jones. This attention to detail not only makes the whole item appear more professionally finished; it is also easier than trying to leave the lid interior perfectly flat.

4

Roughly shape the outside of the lid.

5

Next, mount the other half of the blank and cut a 25mm (1") long spigot.

6

Chase a 16tpi thread to fit the lid, making sure that the thread is not so tight as to hinder later release. If the lid does not screw and unscrew easily you will experience great difficulty in removing this threaded insert when you come to finishing it later. It is important to make this threaded spigot longer than you initially need, hence the recommended 25mm (1"), so that later on the part remaining can be used for remounting the lid for finishing its top surface. The eventual diameter will be smaller than the thread, so there is no unnecessary wastage. It is also important to remember to partly hollow the spigot end, to prevent fouling by any pattern you may have applied to the inside of the lid.

7

With the lid screwed on, mark the parting point.

8

Hollow the end of this spigot to take the collar of box, as shown in the diagram on p 31 and the picture above.

9

Part to the depth of the lid recess for finishing in the next process. This becomes the revolving collar, essential to the operation of the puzzle.

10

For now leave the remainder of thread for remounting the lid later. Note the pencil marks used so that the blank can be replaced in the chuck in exactly the same place.

11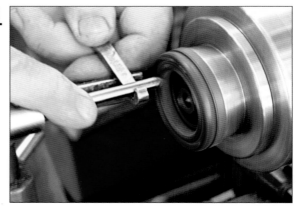

Remount the lid, with its threaded insert and turn very carefully to shape, as in the diagram, then finish the underside of the lid.

12

Having remounted it, you can now screw the lid onto what remains of your spigot to enable finishing of the lid top. The pattern you use on the lid top is your choice; I normally do something similar to what is shown here. Why not customize your box with an inlay or decoration of your own choice?

13

The remainder of the blank needs to be reduced to the diameter of the larger aperture in the threaded insert. Allowing a small collar of this diameter (see the diagram) the remainder can be reduced to the diameter of the hole in the insert.

14

Hollow out the box interior. Turn to either shape shown in the diagram, or to any shape which allows the box section to pass through the hole in the threaded insert.

15

It is necessary to cut a scrapwood spigot on which this box can then be mounted to enable satisfactory finishing of its base.

I usually apply two coats of sanding sealer and then paste wax, with a final buffing of carnuba wax to finish, but depending on the wood lacquering may be advisable, as the satisfying object you have created is likely to be well handled by all your friends trying to get the lid off.

Enjoy making this elegant, simple puzzle, and remember, the shape of the lid and box can be varied to your own taste.

SOLUTION

Grip the box in your left hand with thumb and forefinger pressing firmly underneath the lid while your right hand unscrews the lid.

The Balls and Chain Puzzle

The object of this puzzle is to remove the chain from the spindle, at each end of which is attached a revolving 'ball'.

This very elegant puzzle can be made in any combination of light and dark wood. For the 'balls' I normally use Box, an unparalleled timber for chasing crisp threads. The spindle here is of African Blackwood, though I have used Satine Bloodwood which also looks good. I do not use Ebony as the spindle needs threads which are too fine for so coarse-grained a wood.

My assumption is that if you are going to try making these puzzles you will already have your own range of tools and mastered the skills necessary to use them. This naturally includes the use of thread chasers, which are essential for almost all of the puzzles I make. The purpose of this book is to provide inspiration for interesting turning projects, not to act as a basic instructional manual, of which there are already many good examples.

Where I quote a certain tpi this is what I normally use, but it can be altered to suit your own implements. For the small threads I use a 3/16" Whitworth tap for the female threads. The male ones I always do with a 24 tpi chaser as a die will all too easily break off the spigot on which it is being used.

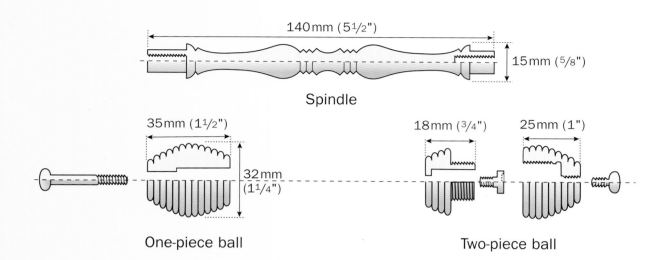

140mm (5½")

15mm (⅝")

Spindle

35mm (1½")

32mm (1¼")

One-piece ball

18mm (¾")

25mm (1")

Two-piece ball

1

Turn a cylinder in boxwood 32mm (1¼") diameter and 82mm (3¼") long. This size will be held in most chucks. My preference is for the Vicmarc 100 with the original jaws, which hold most of the work I do.

2

Part-off 35mm (1⅜") from the chuck and drill a 10mm (⅜") hole to a depth of 22mm (⅜")

3

Drill through the remaining depth a hole 6mm (¼") in diameter. This will be the non-operative end but the ball must still revolve freely.

4

Mount the remaining piece and part-off at 25mm (1") taking care, if the wood has attractive markings, to ensure grain pattern compared with the first piece. This is to ensure that both ends look as if they are from the same piece of wood. To neglect this will mean the end result is not so pleasing, and these puzzles must not only baffle and work well, they must also look good.

5

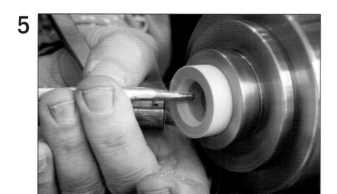

Hollow the piece (it will form the larger, outer half of this two-piece ball) to a depth and diameter of 16 mm ($^5/8$") to enable an 18 tpi female thread to be cut to accept the other half of the ball.

6

Now cut a spigot for a matching 18 tpi thread on the other half of the ball.

7

This should fit well, but very definitely not tightly, into the last thread you cut. The grain flow of these two pieces is of paramount importance. Achieve this by a combination of patiently removing a little from the back shoulder of the spigot, and taking a whisker off the male thread. Patience will give you the result you are looking for.

8

Hollow the interior of this ball ready to accept a captive retaining screw as shown in the diagram on p 38.

9

Screw the halves of the 'working ball' together and drill a 10 mm ($^3/8$") hole right through the inner end only, to take the end of the spindle. To turn the final beehive shape and finish the balls, each in turn mounted between centres, I use a small wooden jam chuck as shown above.

The join in the screwed together ball should be one of the lines of the pattern. This makes it all but invisible, hence increasing the difficulty in solving the puzzle.

10

Now turn the one-piece ball to a similar shape.

Now finish this ball.

11

In each end of a 140 mm (5 1/2") long, 15 mm (5/8") diameter Blackwood (or Satine Bloodwood) spindle, drill a hole and tap a 3/16" Whitworth thread, à la Bill Jones, about 16 mm (5/8") deep.

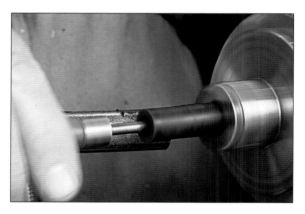

This needs to be done at this stage, as once the spigots are cut to their final size it is very easy for them to split when tapping in this manner.

12

On each end now cut a spigot, one 16 mm (5/8"), and one 10 mm (3/8") long. These spigots must fit easily into the 10 mm (3/8") holes you have made for them in the balls. The shorter spigot should just protrude through its hole into the inner recess of the two-piece ball.

13

From a 60 mm (2 3/8") long 10 mm (3/8") diameter Blackwood rod first turn a spigot and cut 24 tpi thread to fit into the shorter spigot of the main spindle. Part off a 'head' as shown in the diagram.

40

14

On this head form a slot, with which to screw it home in final assembly.

15

Turn a spigot to fit into the outer end of the two-piece ball, and fix either with glue or a screw thread. I naturally prefer the thread.

16

From the remainder of the 10 mm (³/₈") rod cut one last spigot for a 24 tpi thread to fit through the plain ball and into the spindle so that it can rotate freely when screwed up tightly. A touch of cyanoacrylate adhesive ('Superglue') will ensure it does not unscrew once the puzzle is finished.

17

These 24 tpi threaded items can then each be mounted in a ³/₁₆" Whitworth home-made box-wood or bone chuck to be finished to shape. This is so commonly used a size that it is worth making a bone one which will last your lifetime for any further such jobs.

18 Lastly, make a chain which is too small to pass over either ball when assembled. I normally use silver, which for the amount needed is not too dear. The chain must be long enough to pass over the inner part of the two-piece ball. This puzzle, like most of them, is not only fun to make, but also fun to try on your friends.

SOLUTION

Take the spindle in your left hand and, with thumb and forefinger, grip the base of the screwed ball. With the right hand unscrew the end of the ball, thus enabling chain to be easily removed.

The Invisible Gift

The object of this simple, intriguing puzzle is to remove the coin from within.

I usually use Violet Rosewood, Cocobolo or some other such dark, attractively grained wood. The puzzle in the following illustrations is made in Violet Rosewood.

Start with a cylinder about 64 mm (2¹/₂") long and 70 mm (2³/₄") in diameter. Leave sufficient wood on one half to make the spigot for the male thread. The remaining central portion, once reduced in diameter will form the tight-fitting, central bung. Using the blank in this way ensures the grain match necessary to help conceal the bung when it is in position.

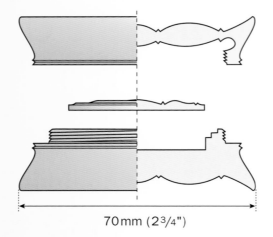

70mm (2¾")

1 Cut a spigot on the blank, pre-marked for parting. The shaded middle band will produce the bung, so that grain can be matched.

2 Part-off one end. The spigot for the male thread is clearly shown here.

3 Form a holding spigot on the middle piece; this will become the bung.

4 Part-off the middle piece.

5

Hollow the lid section.

6

Add pattern as desired to the interior of the lid.

7

Prepare a recess for the female thread.

8

Chase the female thread in the lid.

9

Polish the interior of the lid.

10

Turn a taper for the male thread.

11

A wax ring is clearly showing on the outer end of tapered spigot. This marks the correct diameter for the male thread.

12

Chase the male thread.

13

Now add a quarter cove to the start of the male thread.

14

With the lid screwed on shaping can now be completed.

15

When shaping is complete remove the lid-holding spigot.

16

Add your pattern to the outside surface of the lid.

17

Sand exterior down to 1200 grit.

18

Polish the exterior.

19

Hollow the interior of the base, as shown in the diagram.

20

Now polishing the interior.

21

Next move on to the bung. Reduce the diameter of the middle section saved for the bung.

22

Finally, and very carefully, dimension the central bung. This has to be extremely accurate.

23

With the bung in place, finish the internal surfaces. This helps the deception.

24

Exact dimensions are not given as each part needs to be made a custom fit in each puzzle.

Remove the base spigot.

25

26

Now pattern the base in a similar manner to the lid.

To finish the box, sand and finish the base to match the other parts.

SOLUTION

*Simply tap the base on one hand, or on a suitable surface, whilst holding the box firmly in your other hand. The coin inside then pushes off the bung. **Caution:** always make certain that there is a coin inside prior to fitting the bung in place. Without the coin the lid will not come off.*

The Wedding Ring Box

The puzzle here is to find the hidden wedding ring.

This attractive and functional puzzle is a similar shape to the Invisible Gift. I normally use Papua New Guinea Ebony, which, with its contrasting grain pattern, shows off the puzzle extremely well. The design is of medium difficulty as the fitting of the internal box requires great accuracy.

Once the box is made it only remains to fit a ring over the small internal spigot before assembly. You could make the ring yourself or use a bought one. Sterling silver rings can be purchased quite inexpensively from your local jeweller, or perhaps the box is to be made expressly to help present a special ring.

Whatever it is made for, the Wedding Ring Box will not only enhance its precious contents but also add to the fun as the recipient searches to find a way in to their gift.

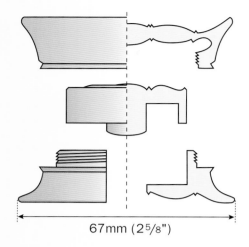

67mm (2⁵/₈")

1 Form a cylinder 67 mm (2⁵/₈") in diameter and 64 mm (2¹/₂") long, with a short holding spigot at each end.

2 Part this blank at 19 mm (³/₄") and hollow it to a depth of about 10 mm (³/₈") and a diameter of 51 mm (2").

3 Shape the inside surface to match the diagram, or to a pattern of your choice.

4 Chase a 16 tpi thread and finish the inside of the lid.

5

Switching to the opposite end of the blank, part-off at 22 mm ($^7/_8$ ”), cut a 7.5 mm ($^5/_{16}$ ”) spigot.

6

Chase a 16 tpi thread to match the one inside the lid. This should be a good fit and also allow the grain to match as nearly as possible.

7

Screw on the lid and turn it to the shape shown in the diagram, or according to your own design, then finish.

8

Remove the lid and drill a hole 13 mm ($^1/_2$ ”) in diameter right through and hollow the rest of the base to take the internal box, as shown in the diagram.

9

Now take the remaining piece of the blank. First make sure the grain direction matches the base into which it will fit. Reduce in diameter to a tight fit within the base section.

Hollow on the underside as shown in the diagram, leaving the spigot a tight fit in the pre-drilled 13 mm ($^1/_2$") hole. Now sand and finish.

10

Providing the fit is good, the top of this part, fixed firmly inside the base, can be turned to a shape similar to the inside of the lid.

11

From some scrap wood form a chuck onto which the base can be screwed firmly to enable the bottom to be shaped and finished.

12

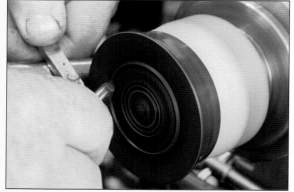

Using the chuck you have made, finish the bottom to the pattern you desire and finish it.

SOLUTION Unscrew the box and carefully press central boss on the base, forcing ring section to reveal itself.

The Castle Money Box

The object of this puzzle is to recover coins from the inside of the castle

This is the original, and first, Castle Money Box.

Having put in your coins they can only be extricated by the use of a further coin, partially inserted, into the slot to unscrew the lid. This baffled some people and these boxes were made in large quantities, mostly in boxwood, during the nineteenth and early part of the twentieth centuries. The following two chapters give details of two developments of the Castle Money Box idea.

Boxwood particularly lends itself to this box, as it makes such a beautifully finished article. Most modern boxwood has at least some grey fungal staining, which I personally think adds character to the wood, but if it does not appeal to you, then either find a perfectly clear piece, or choose another wood.

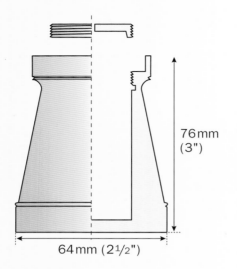

76mm
(3")

64mm (2¹/₂")

A branch log of boxwood, prior to turning.

Rough out the blank to about 64mm (2¹/₂").

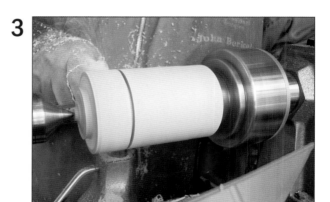

Part-off 76mm (3") from the chuck.

Once it has been shaped add some rings to the body of the castle.

Next start hollowing the top.

6

Complete hollowing down to 70 mm (2³/₄").

7

Chase a 20 tpi female thread into the top of the body recess.

8

Cut the castellations, à la Bill Jones, with a cutting disc held in the chuck. This process can be more laboriously undertaken with a fine-toothed saw.

9

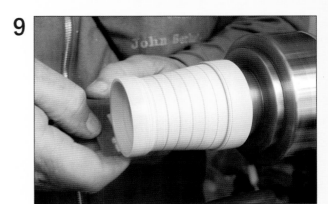

Sand the finished castle body right down to 1200 grit.

10

Mount the remainder of the original blank in the chuck and, having shaped the top, chase a matching male 20 tpi thread.

11

Hollow the inside of the lid, so that the top is not too thick.

12

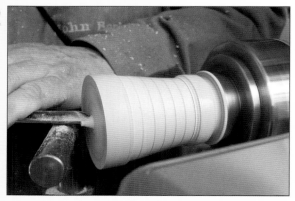

With the body screwed onto the lid the body's bottom spigot can now be removed.

13

Finish the bottom and polish it.

14

The lid can now be parted.

15

Next cut the slot. It will always be necessary to finish this process with a file, as the rotary cutter does not get right up to the outside corners. Cutting this slot is my least favourite process, and one in which a small slip renders the lid useless.

16

With the slot now cut, polish the lid. This removes any sharp edges.

SOLUTION

The puzzle in this money box is simply solved – once it is realized that the top 'floor' can be unscrewed. Naturally, a coin makes an ideal screwdriver when half-inserted into the slot.

The New Castle Money Box

The object of this puzzle is to recover coins from the inside of the castle

The original Castle Money Box (see previous chapter) is an attractive money box in the shape of a chess castle, with a slot cut in the flat lid, which simply screws into the top of the castle.

This first design was followed, before Louis Hoffmann's book was published in 1893, by the New Castle Money Box. Despite any phonetic connection it was not devised in Newcastle!

The New Castle Money Box involves the use of a simple locking pin. I have rendered the pin much more secure by making it captive. The captive pin needs a thicker wall to accommodate it, but prevents the pin being lost, which must have been a continual source of annoyance when they were originally made. This box is made more in the shape of a Staunton pattern chess castle than the original Castle. The puzzle's shape and wood, Santos Rosewood, were chosen by Donald Goddard. However, great care must be taken when using Santos Rosewood as it can sometimes cause an allergic reaction. I often use She-oak, which is more user-friendly, and have used it for the puzzle illustrated here.

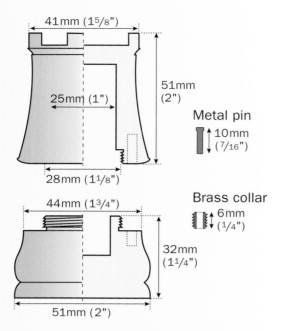

41mm (1⁵/₈")

51mm (2")

25mm (1")

28mm (1¹/₈")

Metal pin
10mm (⁷/₁₆")

44mm (1³/₄")

Brass collar
6mm (¹/₄")

32mm (1¹/₄")

51mm (2")

1

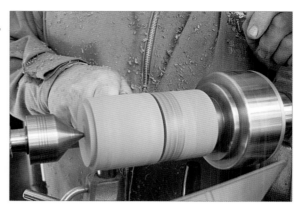

Form a cylinder 51mm (2") in diameter and 95mm (3") long, with a holding spigot on each end. Part the blank at 51mm (2").

2

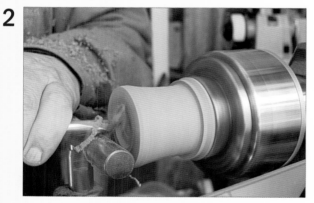

Hollow the larger section to 25mm (1") in diameter and 38mm (1¹/₂") deep, leaving sufficient meat in the walls to accept a ³/₁₆" Whitworth-threaded captive locking pin.

3

Widen the entrance to the hole a little to 8mm (1¹/₂") depth, then chase a 16 tpi female thread inside.

4

Mount the smaller part of the blank, cut a spigot and chase a 16 tpi thread to fit the top half. Take particular care to line up the grain pattern, or the solution to the puzzle will be too obvious. The bottom half can now be hollowed Inside, if you wish, then this and the thread can be finished.

5

Screw the bottom and top halves firmly together to enable them to be turned to shape.

58

6

Hollow the top prior to cutting the castellations.

7

Cut out the six equally spaced castellations. I use a hub cutter, which you can easily make for yourself (see Bill Jones' writings), as I find it so much quicker, though you can of course use a fine-toothed saw.

8

At this point one of my least favourite jobs has to be done. The slot through which the money goes, has to be cut in the top surface. I have found this best done (but not quickly I should point out) by drilling a row of holes, the serrated edges of which are then painstakingly filed straight. It is not practical to use a circular cutter for this purpose. The whole operation could be done with a small router.

9

Drill a hole in the bottom face of the top half to take the 3/16" Whitworth-threaded captive locking pin. Drill a corresponding hole in the lower half for it to lock into. The position for this can be marked by shaking a temporary loose pointed pin up and down with some vigour, or by accurate measurement.

10

Tap the upper half with a hand held engineers 3/16" Whitworth tap. It has other wood turning uses if mounted on a wooden handle.

11

To make the brass locking pin with its retaining collar, drill a 3/16" Whitworth-threaded piece of brass rod.

12

Cut a screw slot into the studding to enable its positioning.

13

Before screwing it in to the bottom face of the top half, fit into it a small, loose-fitting, brass, nail-headed pin, which is easily turned from a short length of $1/8$" brass brazing rod.

14

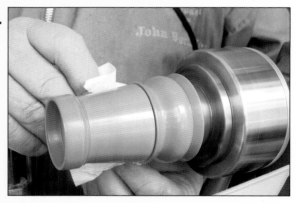

The assembled puzzle can now be finished to your satisfaction. I use either sanding sealer and paste wax or Chestnut friction polish. All of these puzzles can be even further improved by buffing on the lathe with lustre polish, and then with carnuba wax.

15

Remount the base section on a scrap wood screw chuck to enable you to finish off the base by the same process as used to finish the body.

SOLUTION

Tip the puzzle upside down, release pin and give the puzzle a sharp tap to persuade the pin to fall into the top half. The box can now be unscrewed.

The New New Castle Money Box

The object of this puzzle, as with the other 'castle' money boxes, is to gain access to the contents of the castle

This is the third of the Castle Money Box series and this one I myself designed. The idea came to me, as ideas often do, one night whilst in bed. It is of a slightly different design to the previous two. I normally use African Blackwood for this box. It is the most taxing of the trio to solve, but like all of these puzzles it is easy once you know how.

I find the best sequence for its construction is as illustrated in the following pages.

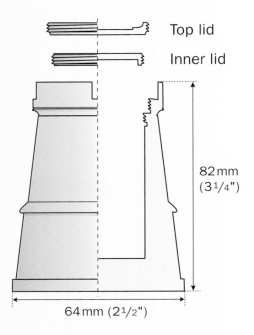

Top lid

Inner lid

82 mm
(3¼")

64 mm (2½")

1 First rough out a 64 mm (2½") blank. I use instrument bell blanks for this box. Mark off at 82 mm (3¼") from the chuck, leaving remaining 8 mm (5/16") for the top lid, Part-off this lid section, then roughly shape the outside of the body.

2

Add rings as a pattern to the body.

3

Carefully shape the body.

4

Now hollow the top of the body.

5

Drill the body to establish the correct depth of hole, 70 mm (2¾").

6

Now hollow the body to the full depth, and to the shape shown in the diagram. Exact dimensions are arbitrary.

7

Chase a 20 tpi right-hand female thread in the lower thread recess. Chasing the left-hand thread then follows, but since the process looks identical only one photo is shown.

8

Mark the rim for the castellation depth and for the position of the six cuts are needed.

9

The cutter used to make the castellations.

10

Cut the castellations as for the New Castle Money Box.

11

A Blackwood blank (no need to match for grain) is now prepared for the right-hand male thread. This becomes the inner lid.

12 The spigot has been tapered, and shows the wax witness mark used for thread diameter.

13 Chase a 20 tpi male thread onto the edge of the inner lid.

14 Turn off the spigot left on the top of the inner lid. This allows the top lid to be made a flush fit.

15 Shape the top lid next, from the remainder of original blank so that it has the same grain and colour as the body.

16 Chase a 20 tpi male thread on the edge of the top lid.

17 Shape the top of the top lid. Remember that left-hand threads unscrew easily, so carefully take light cuts.

18

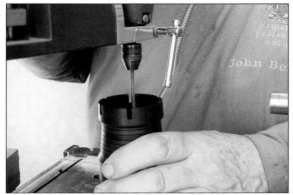

Drill a row of holes through both lids, once they have been screwed firmly on top of each other. Finish by filing the hole sides straight. Because of the depth below the castellations it is not practical to use the disc cutter for this purpose.

19

The puzzle can now be finished, down to 1200 grit...

20

... and polished.

21

With the body firmly screwed onto a scrap wood chuck, remove the base-holding spigot.

22

Finally finish the bottom...

23

... and polish it.

SOLUTION *The box can be opened only by inserting a very small amount of a coin to unscrew the top lid first in one direction, then the lower lid in the opposite direction.*

The Egyptian Box

The object of the Egyptian Box is too remove a coin from within.

Why The Egyptian Box is so called I do not know. I should love to hear of any ideas as to why. This puzzle has been devised from a puzzle called 'The New Brass Puzzle Match Box'. Of course it was originally made in brass, and held matches. I have converted its principle and workings to a wooden one to hold coins, not matches. I normally make this box from Red Lancewood, a very attractive Australian wood. Like most of these puzzles it is a classic exercise in hand thread chasing.

It is the case with all of the puzzles presented in this book that the dimensions are merely those taken from a puzzle I have made; they can be changed to suit the size of blank you have to start with, keeping the proportions similar. Similar flexibility can be applied to the thread sizes. This is one of the twelve puzzles which I make in miniature.

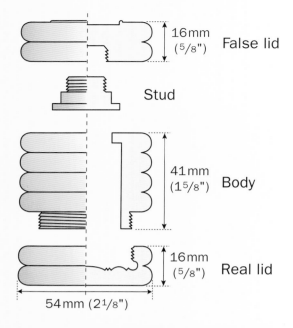

False lid — 16mm (5/8")

Stud

Body — 41mm (1 5/8")

Real lid — 16mm (5/8")

54mm (2 1/8")

1

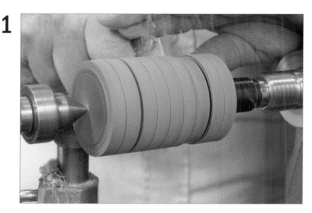

Form a cylinder 54 mm (2 1/8") in diameter and 80 mm (3 1/8") long to allow extra for spigots if this diameter will not fit your chuck. Part at 16 mm (5/8"), and mark at 58.5 mm (2 1/4"). These dimensions allow for roughly 8 mm (5/16") beads and 1.5 mm (1/16") parting tools.

2

Hollow out the 16 mm (5/8") section, as with the lid of any box.

3

Chase a 16 tpi left-handed thread, and finish as in diagram. This will be the base of the box. I normally finish bases with a few concentric rings, which make it look as if you have taken a little extra care in finishing. Left-hand threads are done in exactly the same way as right-hand ones, with the exception of the direction of traverse of the chaser, which is moved clockwise, instead of anticlockwise (for male threads).

4

Clean out any wax left in the thread with an old toothbrush.

5

On the adjoining end of the large piece, form a spigot on which to cut a 16 tpi male thread to match that on the base you have just finished.

6

Chase a 16 tpi left-hand thread to fit accurately. Be sure to achieve a good grain match with the lid/bottom as the whole success of this puzzle depends on this one factor.

7

Now, with the lid/bottom screwed on tightly, finish the lid, making it look like the bottom. Care has to be taken with this process as, being a left-hand thread, it is liable to unscrew, so take very light cuts. This piece is now finished.

8

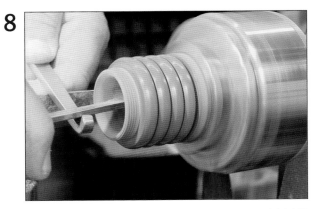

Hollow the box body to a depth of 38 mm (1 1/2") to accept your coins, and to a 16 mm (5/8") diameter to a depth of 48 mm (1 7/8").
The diagram better helps to make the reasons for this clear.

9

The outside of the body can now be finished with 8 mm (5/16") beads as in the diagram and parted at the previously marked point.

10

Hollow the section you parted-off earlier, which will actually be the top, to a full depth of 10 mm (3/8") and a diameter of 14 mm (9/16").

11

Chase a 16 tpi thread into the hollowed top.

12

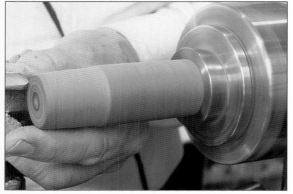

From a blank which will fit into the main body of the box, and which is able to revolve freely therein, but not necessarily of the same wood, cut a spigot and chase a 16 tpi thread to screw into the last thread you chased on the box lid.

13

With the lid screwed onto this blank its outside can now be finished with two more beads.

14

Cut a recess on the top to take any coin of your choosing.

15

Form an attractive pattern on the head of the holding stud.

16

The blank needs to be adjusted so that, when tightly screwed into the lid section through the bottom of the box, the lid can freely revolve in both directions without it unscrewing. Part off the 'business end' of the blank, and finish it's top surface.

All that now remains is for you to assemble this most attractive and intriguing puzzle and try it out on your friends.

SOLUTION

The lid with the coin on it merely revolves in both directions, but the bottom two rings unscrew from the body with a left-hand thread to release the coin.

The New 'Brass' Puzzle

The object of this puzzle is to remove the coin through the coin slot, without unscrewing the lid from the base.

This puzzle is so named because the original was made in brass. The shape is not the same as the original and can be varied to suit your own taste. I normally make it in She-oak, which cuts adequate threads. Like many of the projects in this collection it is an improved version of a puzzle from a book by Professor Louis Hoffmann published in 1893.

I do not try to give instruction on which tools to select, and how to use them, as this is already covered by others before me, particularly the master Bill Jones, from whose writings virtually all my knowledge and inspiration have come.

The measurements I quote are for your guidance; they can be varied to suit your pieces of wood, but the proportions should stay about the same.

The slot and hole in the lid can be made to fit any coin you like. I normally use a two-pence piece. As always with these puzzles, following the simple steps to make it provides you not only with the fun of doing so, but the satisfaction afterwards of trying it out on your friends.

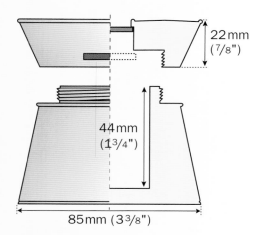

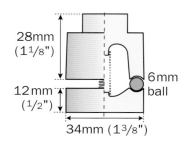

22mm
(^{7}/$_8$")

44mm
(1^3/$_4$")

85mm (3^3/$_8$")

28mm
(1^1/$_8$")

12mm
(^{1}/$_2$")

6mm
ball

34mm (1^3/$_8$")

1

Turn a cylinder of She-oak 85mm (3^3/$_8$") in diameter and cut a holding spigot at each end. Part off at 22mm (^{7}/$_8$") from the chuck.

2

This part will form the lid of the box, so hollow to a depth of 10mm (^{3}/$_8$").

3

Chase a 16tpi thread. Whilst still held in the chuck, drill right through a hole slightly *smaller* than the coin you intend to use, and shape as in the diagram. Make all but the last 3mm (^{1}/$_8$") large enough for the coin to fit.

4

Now fix the larger piece in your chuck and cut a spigot.

5

Chase on it a 16 tpi thread to accept the lid of the box. This should allow the lid to fit without force and should be made so that the grain patterns line up. You need patience to achieve this, but with judicious removal of wood from the back wall of the spigot it is easily done. Remember that one whole turn of 16 tpi, is equivalent to $1/16$", so a half turn needs $1/32$" removed, and so on. Err on the side of caution lest you go too far.

6

Screw on the lid and cut behind the hole, a recess which just fits your coin. Do this so that the coin is visible as near to the surface as possible, while still being held captive.

7

The whole of the outside can now be turned to shape and finished in the manner you prefer.

I normally use two coats of sanding sealer and Chestnut Clear Woodwax 22. This is a toluene-free wax, a quick drying blend of beeswax and carnuba wax which can be used on any wood without discoloration.

8

Having got that bit over with you should next hollow the box to a depth of 44 mm ($1^3/4$") and diameter of 35 mm ($1^3/8$").

9

Now for the mechanism. Part-off a 35 mm ($1^3/8$") long boxwood blank, 12 mm ($1/2$") from the end in the chuck and shape as in the diagram. Cut a recess to accept a 6 mm ($1/4$") ball bearing and a central spigot to hold a small spring.

10

Mount the remainder of the blank and, as with the lower half, shape as in diagram to accept the ball and spring. Make sure it is a loose fit in the box as it needs to slide up and down freely.

11

Re-mount the box with its lid fitted. Careful measurement is needed to determine the exact line on which to cut the coin slot so that the mechanism blocks it when the ball is in place but clears it without the ball. Drill a row of 3mm ($^1/8$") holes on this line, long enough to allow your coin to pass through. Finish this slot carefully with a file and abrasive.

12

Make a scrap wood chuck with a 16tpi thread onto which you can screw the body of the box, or carefully grip it in small expansion jaws to enable finishing of its base. Now finish the base.

All that remains is to assemble the box and try it out on your friends. I usually use a 5mm diameter spring (see Proops and Pollards in List of Suppliers). Strength can be varied by adjusting its length. Neither diameter nor strength are critical. Its purpose is to keep the coin at the top of the internal box except when pressed.

SOLUTION

The ball bearing normally sits on the rim inside and prevents the coin from being extracted through the slot. Invert box, give it a gentle shake to allow ball to fall into inner recess, and this allows depression of coin sufficient for it to be extracted through the slot. The screwed on lid is just for assembly and must not be used to extricate coin.

The Ball and Three Strings

The object of this attractive puzzle is to remove the small balls without untying the knots that retain them.

This puzzle is made in Box and Walnut, with Blackwood balls. It is one of the most elegant of puzzles and gives the puzzler plenty to think about when trying to solve it. I construct the body from three screwed sections simply to make it easier to thread the strings when assembling, and reassembling the puzzle. The puzzle-solver should not unscrew the puzzle, but to do so does not actually help much in its solution. The whole puzzle can also be made in miniature.

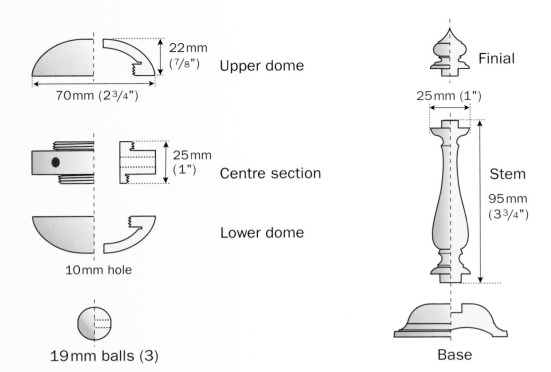

22mm (⁷/₈") — Upper dome

70mm (2³/₄")

Finial

25mm (1")

25mm (1") — Centre section

Stem

95mm (3³/₄")

Lower dome

10mm hole

19mm balls (3)

Base

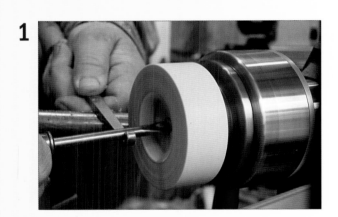

1 Turn a boxwood cylinder 70mm (2³/₄") in diameter, 44mm (1³/₄") long and cut a holding spigot on each end.

Part at 22mm (⁷/₈") from chuck. Drill a 10mm (³/₈") hole right through and hollow a 44mm (1³/₄") hole to a depth of 7.5mm (⁵/₁₆"), shaping the remaining cavity as in the diagram.

Chase a 16tpi female thread around its inner edge.

It is important, at this stage, to wax this thread you have just cut.

4

Turn a 70 mm (2³/₄") diameter by 50 mm (2") long blank, in Walnut or any other contrasting wood, and cut a 4.5 mm (1/8") long holding spigot on one end.

5

Part at 25 mm (1") from the chuck, then cut a 4.5 mm (³/₁₆") spigot and chase on it a thread to match one boxwood dome.

6

Hollow the inside of the central section right through.

7

Re-chuck the other boxwood dome and do the same, except make the hollow a little smaller – say, 38 mm (1¹/₂"). This difference prevents any subsequent incorrect assembly.

8

Screw one dome to the central section and mount the boxwood end in your chuck. Now cut a spigot and chase a thread on the other end of the central section to match the other boxwood dome.

9

Drill three 6 mm (1/4") holes equidistant around the centre line of the central section and finish.

10

Working between centres now, turn all three pieces, screwed together, into the requisite 'near-spherical' shape.

11

Sand and polish the whole of the large ball.

12

From a piece of Walnut turn the stand for the base. Exact size will depend on your Walnut blank, (you could use the remaining part of the central section blank, reduced in diameter) and is not too critical, though it should be smaller than the diameter of the ball.

13

From a 95 mm (3³/₄") long and 25 mm (1") diameter Walnut blank, turn a stem, as shown in the diagram.

14

From a similar piece of wood turn the finial, again following the diagram.

15

From a 19 mm (³/₄") diameter blackwood blank, turn three balls. First drill through each a 4.5 mm (³/₁₆") hole as it will then be easier to turn these balls between centres.

16

Chamfer the holes at each end.

17

Turn the balls to shape and finish them.

Thread two balls onto a 342 mm (13½") length of cord, doubled and knotted together at the loose end. The third ball has two separate ends passed through as pictured below.

Now the fun of combining the strings; this is best done following the picture below. Two strings are knotted together at their ends, the third ends in two separate knots. A very elegant teaser for your friends!

SOLUTION

Find the string with two knots and pull so that the two loops emerge. Pass this ball back over the loops. It is now possible to remove all three strings.

The Sceptre Puzzle

The object of the Sceptre puzzle is too remove the ring from the shaft.

This is one of the most elegant of puzzles, especially when it is made in either South American Tulipwood or Kingwood. Because of the number of small 'flowers' there are to make, it takes patience, but that is something which woodturners have in abundance. I have found the best sequence for its construction to be as it is described in the next five pages.

The shape of the ends here is similar to the Victorian original, but they can be made to any design of your choice. The ring and flowers could equally be made in bone or 'alternative ivory', which provide a good contrast against the different coloured woods that make up the balls and spindle.

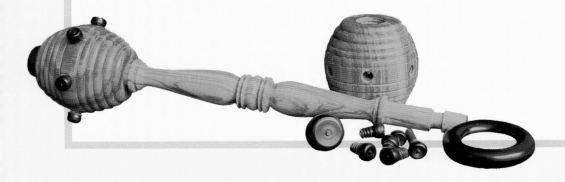

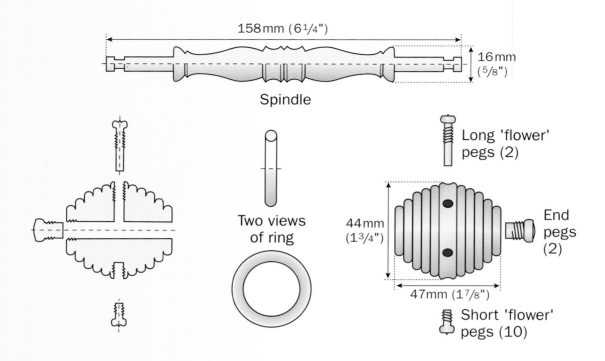

158mm (6¼")

16mm (⅝")

Spindle

Two views of ring

Long 'flower' pegs (2)

44mm (1¾")

47mm (1⅞")

End pegs (2)

Short 'flower' pegs (10)

1

Turn a cylinder 44mm (1¾") diameter and 95mm (3¾") long.

2

Part into two equal halves, and drill a 7.5mm (⁵⁄₁₆") hole right through each half.

3

Into the outer end of each hole chase a thread of whatever size you choose.

4

Shape each ball in turn, between centres, as shown in the diagram.

5

Make a scrap wood chuck with a thread to match that in the end of each half of the ball.

6

With each half, in turn, mounted on a scrap wood chuck, mark six points, equally spaced around its 'equator'.

7

Drill six holes at the points you have marked around the central ring. On each ball five of them on need to be 10 mm deep and one must go right through to the central hole.

8

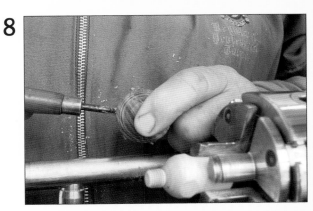

Now tap $^3/_{16}$" Whitworth threads in each hole.

9

Finish as you would normally.

10

On a cylinder about 158 mm (6¼") long and 16 mm (⅝") in diameter cut a 7.5 mm (5/16") spigot to loosely fit the holes in each end ball.

11

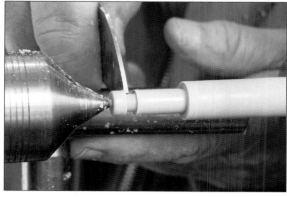

Now cut a notch to depth of a third of the diameter, positioned directly in line with the holes on the ball. This position is easily marked by fitting the ball on the spindle and scribing through the hole that has been drilled right through.

12

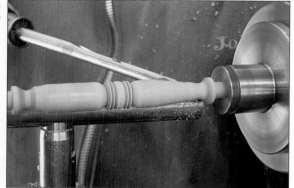

Now turn the spindle to shape between centres,

13

finish and polish the spindle.

14

From a darker wood (I favour African Blackwood) turn and chase with 5/16", 24 tpi threads, ten small 'flowers' as shown in the diagram.

15

Also make the two longer flowers, which will retain the ball ends on the finished spindle. Shape their heads to exactly match the short 'flowers' , rendering their threaded ends as shown in the diagram.

16

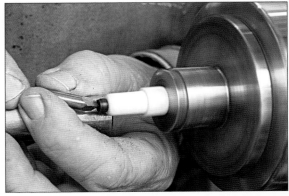

All the flowers can have their heads finished in a small, custom-made chuck.

17

Make two Blackwood end pegs, with threads chased to match the holes in the sceptre ends. Note the wax marked ring on the end of the tapered spigot, denoting the correct diameter for the thread.

18

Now chase a thread on each end peg to match that in each end piece.

19

After parting the end peg can be carefully held in a chuck for finishing.

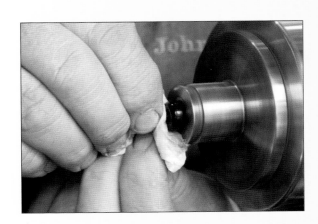

20

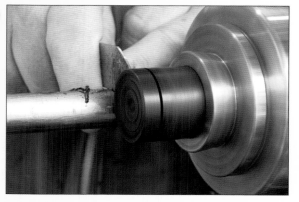

Lastly make a Blackwood ring to easily fit over the spindle. The following six pictures describe this process.

SOLUTION

By trial and error find which of the flowers is the long one holding on either end. Unscrewing this flower enables the ring to be removed.

The Lighthouse Puzzle

The object of the Lighthouse Puzzle is too remove the ring from the shaft.

This puzzle is almost certainly the most attractive one that I make and it is one of my favourites. Its flowing lines and elegant combination of colours make it a most suitable adornment to any sideboard or mantlepiece. Add to this the fact that it is a puzzle and you have a real *pièce de résistance*.

The Lighthouse Puzzle is not too difficult to make, it being just a series of thread chasing exercises. I use different threads because I think that it helps the fitting together, but one thread only, say 20 tpi, would work quite satisfactorily. The sequence in which the component parts are best made, in my experience, is as described over the next five pages.

Upper light

Lower light

Body

158mm
(6¼")

Bottom

50mm (2")

Base

Light mid-section

41mm
(1⁵/₈")

38mm (1½")

Finial

Pin

Core

82mm
(3¼")

22mm (⁷/₈")

Two views
of ring

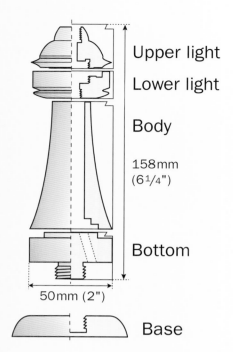

1 First form a cylinder 158mm (6³/₈") long, to allow for parting cuts, and 50mm (2") in diameter. I use Mopane, and part-off with spigots, as shown in the diagram.

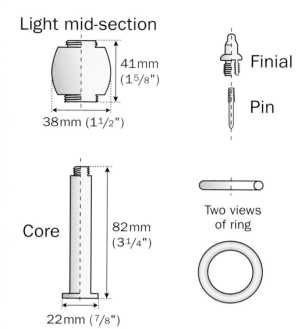

2 Turn a 13mm (¹/₂") Blackwood blank to a diameter of 70mm (2³/₄") with a holding spigot. Hollow the face of this piece to 16mm (⁵/₈") and 10mm (³/₈") deep.

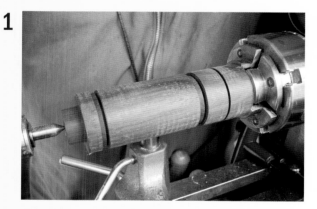

3 Chase a 16tpi thread, shape as in the diagram, and finish.

4 Here the Blackwood base is seen screwed onto the bottom end of the base section.

5

Cut a spigot on the bottom section.

6

Mount the main body section on its spigot and drill a 16 mm ($^5/_8$") hole right through. Shape the lower end of hole as shown in the diagram.

7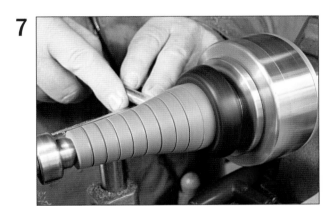

With a tight push fit, mount the body onto the bottom section, which is screwed to the Blackwood base, shape the outside with a gentle taper from 51 mm (2") to 25 mm (1") at the top end. Mark a series of rings 7.5 mm ($^5/_{16}$") apart, and finish.

8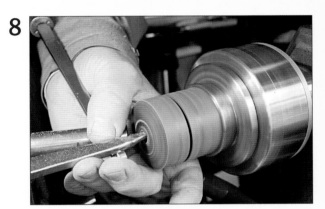

Grip the upper and lower light sections in a chuck and drill a 10 mm ($^3/_8$") hole more than halfway through from the bottom end. At this lower end chase a 20 tpi thread.

9

The two light sections can now be parted.

10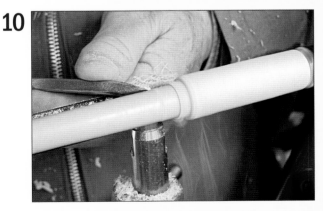

Next make the central core. Turn a 22 mm ($^7/_8$") diameter, 82 mm ($3^1/_4$") long piece of boxwood. Turn a 13 mm ($^1/_2$") spigot, about 70 mm ($2^3/_4$") long on one end of the core.

11

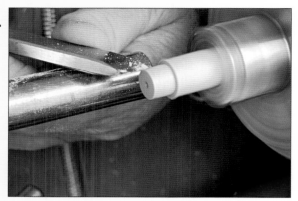

Turn a short spigot on which to cut the thread to screw into the base of the light.

12

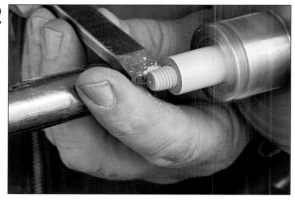

This leaves sufficient diameter for a small shoulder to remain after cutting the 20 tpi thread to fit lower light section.

13

Screw the parted-off lower light section onto the end of this central core. Hollow its internal face 22 mm ($^7/_8$") in diameter and 6 mm ($^1/_4$") deep.

14

Into the recess you have just formed cut a 20 tpi thread.

15

Remount the top light section in the chuck and form a hollow exactly as in bottom light section. This will allow the whole light to screw together when the light mid-section is made. I always make these two internal apertures slightly different sizes so that the light can only be assembled correctly.

16

Now chase a 20 tpi female thread in the top light recess.

17

Turn a boxwood mid-section for the light 38 mm (1¹/₂") in diameter and 41 mm (1⁵/₈") long and chase, on a spigot at each end, 20 tpi threads to allow whole light to be screwed together.

18

This shows the second thread being cut, whilst mid-section is screwed firmly onto the lower light section.

19

Drill a 10 mm (³/₈") hole in top end of light.

20

Now chase an 18 tpi thread for the finial to screw into.

21

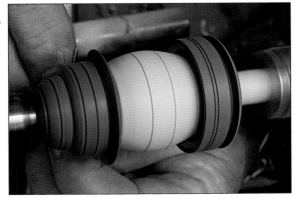

To turn the three light sections to their final shape screw the assembled light onto the central core, whilst it is held firmly in the chuck, and support the top of the light by the tailstock.

22

Using a 25 mm (1") by 13 mm (¹/₂") diameter Blackwood blank, drill and tap a ³/₁₆" Whitworth thread.

23

Once the blank is tapped, turn the finial as in the diagram, and cut an 18 tpi thread to fit the female thread in the top of the upper light section.

24

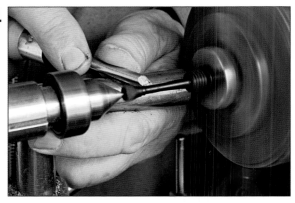

From a 35 mm (1³/₈") by 6 mm (¹/₄") diameter Blackwood blank turn the unlocking pin which must then be chased with a 24 tpi thread to fit the ³/₁₆" threaded hole in the finial's base.

25

Finish the Blackwood base's top surface.

26

Screw the base to the bottom section. Remove the base's holding spigot and finish completely.

27 Drill four equally spaced holes in the bottom section; slant them at about 15° towards the centre. Only one of these should go right through to correspond with a hole in the core. With the inner core in place drill into this too, to enable the peg to immobilize the core when inserted in the correct hole.

28 Lastly, before final assembly, turn a Blackwood ring that fits over the top part of body, but not the bottom (see p 86 for turning a ring).

SOLUTION *Unscrew the locking pin from the finial and remove the base to reveal the four holes. Probe each hole with the pin and find the 'through' hole; the one into which the pin goes furthest. Now, pressing the pin gently into the correct hole, rotate the light until the pin locates in the hole. This allows the core to be held steady while the light is unscrewed and the ring removed.*

The New Persian Puzzle

The object of the New Persian Puzzle is to find the ring hidden inside the puzzle.

The reason why this puzzle is so called leaves me completely baffled. Any ideas? I usually make it in Cocobolo, but if you do so, then please take every possible precaution, as Cocobolo is notorious for causing allergies. This wood particularly lends itself to the elegant length of this puzzle. As with all of these puzzles, measurements can be varied, though because it conceals a ring, miniaturization is not an option for this one, unless you have fairies with very small fingers at the bottom of your garden.

I have modified the original design so it is little more difficult than the original, both to make and to solve. The original version merely had a knob screwed onto each end of the central spindle.

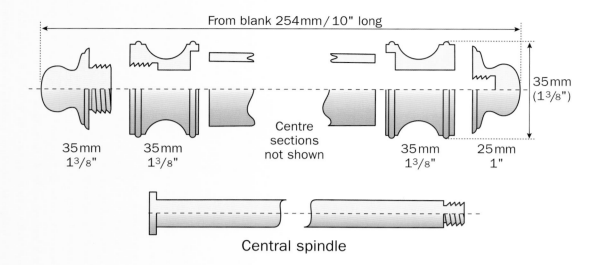

From blank 254mm / 10" long

35mm
(1³/₈")

Centre
sections
not shown

35mm
1³/₈"

35mm
1³/₈"

35mm
1³/₈"

25mm
1"

Central spindle

1 Turn a cylinder 254mm (10") long and 38mm (1¹/₂") in diameter. This length is derived from the length of the blank commonly available, but it can easily be longer if you have such wood at your disposal.

When parting-off, as in the diagram, ensure you mark both the order and the direction of the parts, so that the grain lines up when the puzzle is finished.

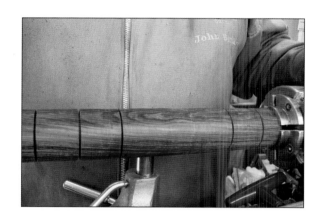

2

3

Hollow right through a diameter of 22mm (⁷/₈"). This leaves enough room inside to take a normal wedding ring. For larger rings this hollow needs to be made to accommodate them and so all the other dimensions will most likely need some adjustment to keep everything in proportion.

Turn the central section to a 32mm (1¹/₄") cylinder. I make the outside diameter of each end of this tube slightly different, so that when the puzzle is assembled it will only go together in the correct order, thus ensuring grain pattern alignment. Held between centres this tube can now be finished in the manner you choose.

4

On the centre-facing ends of the next two pieces form a 3 mm (1/8") deep recess to accept the ends of the cylinder, each to accommodate only the correct end, and allow free rotation of the cylinder between them.

5

Now drill a 13 mm (1/2") hole through both end pieces.

6

Shape the outer end of only one of them as in the diagram and chase a 16 tpi female thread within the hole you have just made.

7

Turn the outside of these two pieces, mounted between centres, to the shape shown in the diagram and finish in exactly the same way as the tube.

8

Mount one knob piece, cut a spigot, and chase a male thread to fit into the thread made in the end piece in step **6**.

9

Mount the knob on a scrap wood chuck, to enable turning of this knob-shaped part.

10

Mount the other knob piece, drill a 10 mm (³/₈") hole and chase a 16 tpi female thread to take the central rod.

11

Make a scrap wood chuck, with a thread to match the second end knob.

12

Attached to this scrap wood chuck turn the second knob to match the first, and finish. If your lathe has a hollow headstock, the knob can be mounted on the end of the central spindle, which you make next.

13

Make the central retaining spindle as in the diagram, with a 16 tpi thread to accept the knob you have just finished. Carve a fairly deep groove across the head end, to give purchase when solving this puzzle, then finish.

All that is left now is to assemble this attractive puzzle and try it out on your friends.

SOLUTION Unscrew the knob from one end, then with a finger on the head of the spindle, unscrew the other knob, to release all the parts and reveal the captive ring.

The Arabi Gun Puzzle

The object of the Arabi Gun Puzzle is to remove the ball, held in position by a spring, from the barrel.

This is a puzzle for the dedicated enthusiast. It is one of the most complex puzzles that I make: a veritable *tour de force* of thread chasing. But each step is, in itself quite simple. Do not be put off by what appears to be a very difficult exercise. Like many of my puzzles, this one can be made in a variety of sizes. I make a miniature version which is only about 100 mm in length.

I normally use African Blackwood, that king of woods, which lends itself so admirably to the hand chasing of threads. For the miniature ones this is especially important. If you carefully follow the instructions and proceed logically, the end result will more than justify the time taken to produce this lovely puzzle.

The last project gives details for making a 'truck', the carriage on which cannons traditionally ride. Displayed on the truck the Arabi Gun becomes a most attractive ornament, quite apart from it also being a puzzle.

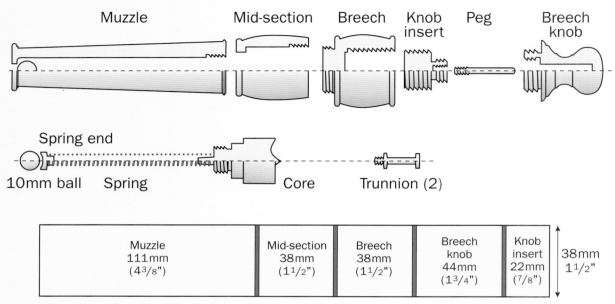

Muzzle   Mid-section   Breech   Knob insert   Peg   Breech knob

Spring end

10mm ball   Spring   Core   Trunnion (2)

Muzzle 111mm (4³/₈")	Mid-section 38mm (1¹/₂")	Breech 38mm (1¹/₂")	Breech knob 44mm (1³/₄")	Knob insert 22mm (⁷/₈")	38mm 1¹/₂"

260mm(10¹/₄") blank; 5mm (¹/₄") allowed for parting cuts

1 Form a cylinder some 38mm (1¹/₂") in diameter and 238mm (9³/₈") long. This allows for four 3mm (¹/₈") parting gaps. Part-off at the dimensions shown in the diagram. Mark each two adjoining pieces to ensure correct grain flow, so that when the gun is finished the joints will be less obvious.

2

I normally work from the muzzle back to the breech knob. It is important to maintain the continuity of grain pattern, so, holding muzzle at the 'open' end, hollow through completely at a diameter of 6mm (¹/₄").

3

Next hollow all but the last 3mm (¹/₈") or so to a diameter of about 16mm (⁵/₈").

98

4

Chase a 16 tpi thread on the opening of the wide, 16 mm (⁵⁄₈") end.

5

At the smaller opening, chamfer the hole internally to allow the ball to sit neatly when the spring holds it at this end.

6

Next make the muzzle-retaining core. From a 25 mm (1") by 44 mm (1³⁄₄") long blank, which can be of another wood (though blackwood is always best) cut a spigot and chase a thread to fit the muzzle. When this is screwed into the muzzle turn the remainder so that it runs true. Cut a 19 mm (³⁄₄") diameter shoulder at the back of the thread so that it will seat in the exit hole of the mid section.

7

The rear end of this core must have a sharp point to prevent cheating when solving the puzzle, by pressing it with a finger. Cut a small spigot at the front end of this part to enable the a spring to be fixed to it later.

8

Chuck the mid section at the muzzle end and hollow right through to a diameter of 19 mm (³⁄₄").

9

Then hollow through a diameter of 25 mm (1") to a depth of 32 mm (1¹⁄₄").

10

Chase a 16 tpi thread at the wide end you have just made. The central core must run freely within this mid section and the muzzle, when screwed tightly onto the core, must also revolve freely.

11

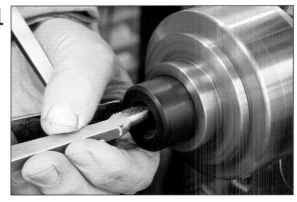

Holding the breech section at its forward end, hollow at a diameter of 19 mm ($3/4$") to a depth of 25 mm (1"). Chase a 16 tpi thread here.

12

Reverse the breech section in the chuck, cut a spigot and chase a thread to fit into the mid section, taking care with this thread to ensure the grain pattern is aligned when screwed up tight into the mid section.

13

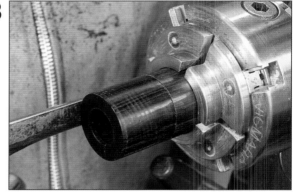

Here are the mid and breech sections, screwed together, showing the grain match.

14

Chuck the last piece, holding at the knob end, and part at 22 mm ($7/8$") from the projecting end to release what will be the knob insert (see diagram).

15

Hollow 6 mm ($1/4$") to a depth of 38 mm ($1 1/2$") to enable the peg to be hidden. Further hollow at a diameter of 10 mm ($3/8$") to a depth of 16 mm ($5/8$") and chase within this an 18 tpi female thread.

16

Roughly shape the knob.

For the next process it may be easier to look at the diagram and picture. Reduce the final piece (knob insert) to 22 mm ($^7/_8$") in diameter. Cut a 16 mm ($^5/_8$") in spigot on what will be it's inner end, then grip it by this spigot.

17

Cut a 13 mm ($^1/_2$") diameter, by 7.5 mm ($^5/_{16}$") long spigot, and chase on it a corresponding 18 tpi thread to fit into the knob.

18

Into this spigot first drill a hole, then tap, a $^3/_{16}$" Whitworth thread to accept the peg, without which it would be impossible to solve this puzzle.

19

Rechuck the knob, screw the two pieces together, then chase a 16 tpi thread to fit into the breech section. Taper this sufficiently so that when it is tightened into the breech, the end does not unscrew.

20

All the pieces, screwed together, can now be finished.

21

Drill two horizontally opposed holes in the mid section for the trunnions to screw into. Only one hole need go right into the core.

22

Tap into both holes a $^3/_{16}$" Whitworth thread.

23

Sand and finish according to your preference.

24

The knob, mounted onto a scrap chuck, can now be finished.

25

The breech knob is completed by making the peg, which is a length of Blackwood about 3mm (1/8") in diameter with a 3/16" Whitworth thread at one end, to fit the corresponding 3/16" thread at the end of the knob.

26

From a 13mm (1/2") blank, form a spring end as in the diagram, to hold the ball in place at the end of the muzzle.

27

On a 10mm (3/8") diameter Blackwood spindle, make a short spigot and cut a 3/16" Whitworth thread to make one of the two trunnions.

28

Reverse this in a small scrap wood 3/16" mandrel and shape each trunnion as in the diagram.

29

Turn a 10mm (3/8") ball from boxwood or bone.

Now assemble the gun and tease your friends!

SOLUTION *Unscrew the trunnions. Unscrew the knob, then unscrew the thread of the knob. Use the peg, thus revealed, to locate in the trunnion hole, enabling the muzzle to be unscrewed.*

The New Jubilee Puzzle

The object of the New Jubilee Puzzle is to find the Queen's head.

This puzzle was originally made around the time of Queen Victoria's Jubilee and was originally made in a simple box shape. Donald Goddard suggested the shape of a beehive would be much more attractive and so I have used this shape ever since making the first one. It poses no real problems and is just an exercise in chasing threads. The wood I normally use is Mgurure. This is a fine African hardwood which takes a beautiful finish. A pale yellow or honey-coloured wood like Box, would also make a very attractive, if rather different, hive.

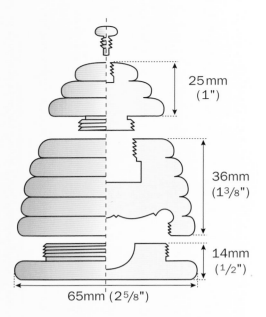

25mm
(1")

36mm
(1³/₈")

14mm
(½")

65mm (2⁵/₈")

1

The blank is 80mm (3¹/₈") long, excluding base spigot, with a diameter of 65mm (2¹/₂"). This allows 5mm (¹/₄") for two parting cuts. To lose as little grain match as possible, use a very thin parting tool. Part from the chuck at 14mm (¹/₂") and then 25mm (1") from the other end.

2

Roughly shape the top and mid sections before they are parted. Next hollow the bottom end of the mid section.

3

Add a recess to this hollow, before chasing a 20tpi female thread in this recess.

4

Chase a matching 20tpi male thread on the bottom section, then remove a small amount from the back shoulder, to allow the grain pattern to line up.

5

Screw the middle and top sections onto the base. The top section can now be rough turned whilst screwed to the base with the middle.

6

Having carefully marked out, incise the sections of the beehive.

7

Part-off the top piece.

8

Hollow the top hole of the mid section. Go as deep as you can without going right through. Next cut a recess for a thread into this hole, and chase a 16 tpi female thread into this. Polishing thread and interior.

9

Having cut a corresponding thread on the lid, now remove a small amount from the shoulder, carefully, to ensure the grain lines up when tightly screwed onto mid section.

10

Assemble all three parts to finish shaping the top.

11

A final shaping of the beehive beads will now probably be in order.

12

Make a hole in the very top to take the final knob. Cut an 18 tpi female thread into it.

13

Sand the whole beehive down to 1200 grit and polish it.

14

Now hollow the inside of the base to accept the topmost ring of the lid for undoing.

15

To complete the base, remove the spigot on its underside.

16

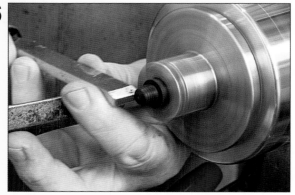

Chase an 18 tpi male thread onto the small African Blackwood knob.

17

To finish the box, shape the top of the knob before polishing it.

SOLUTION

The top section of this puzzle should screw on very tightly. To gain access to the top chamber it is necessary to invert the top into the hollow underneath the base, and use it as a key to unscrew the top, inside which there is a coin bearing the Queen's head.

The Truck

***The object of the truck is to support the Arabi Gun
– there's no puzzle involved here!***

Truck is the name by which the wheeled carriage of a
cannon is traditionally known.

This truck is the carriage on which all three of the
cannons that I make, including the Arabi Gun, are
mounted. It is not too difficult, though I personally do
not enjoy making it as there is too little turning involved.
You might need good glasses for the small pegs, but
otherwise nothing need be a problem.

The addition of this truck makes the very interesting
and complex Arabi Gun puzzle into a most attractive
ornament.

80mm (3¼")

27mm (1⅛")

13mm (½")

8mm (5/16")

8mm (5/16")

40mm (1⅝")

18mm (¾")

10mm (⅜")
pins (4)

5mm (¼") holes

25mm (1") diameter wheel (2)

18mm (¾") diameter wheel (2)

1

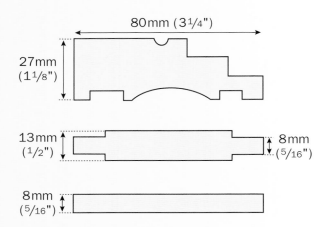

Cut down the wood you are using to give two slices about 7.5 mm (5/16") thick. Mark the pieces shown in the diagram. I normally use some old Jarrah, but Mahogany or Oak would be just as good.

2

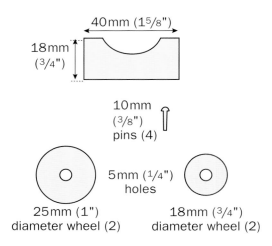

Cut out all the pieces. I normally cut out two sets at time. I use a bandsaw for speed, but a fretsaw will do the job equally well. It is advisable to cut corresponding sides together, so that they are exactly the same. They can easily be fixed together by double-sided tape.

3

Now sand all parts, with reducing grades of abrasive. I use a homemade sanding disc on my lathe. After sanding I normally finish using two coats of sanding sealer, followed by a coat of wax, which is then buffed on the lathe. There are proprietary attachments for this purpose, but it is much more satisfying to make your own 'pigtail' on which to screw your mops.

4

Now for the more interesting part. Working between centres, very carefully turn the axles for all four wheels to a diameter of 5 mm (¼"). I use a miniature two-prong drive, but be careful that the tailstock centrepoint is not tightened so much that the very small spigot splits. It is also possible to use a four-jaw chuck so long as the jaws aperture is small enough.

5 Mark a spot on what will be the top surface, 7.5mm ($5/16$") from the square section, so that when the wheel is fitted it has room to revolve.

Very carefully drill these spots through with a 1.5mm ($1/16$") drill.

6

I use a small, tapered dental burr to taper the holes slightly so the pegs will fit snugly. Now trim any excess from the axle ends and sand them.

7

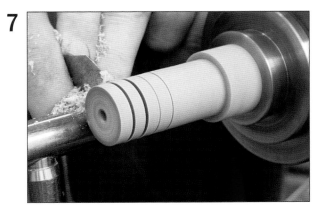

From a piece of wood 4.5mm ($3/16$") thick, which can be either the same or different, turn two pairs of wheels, one 25mm (1") in diameter...

8

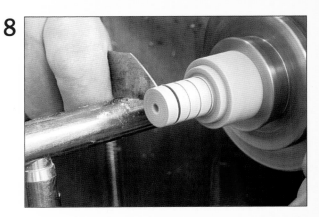

... and one 19mm ($3/4$") in diameter. I normally turn two sets at once to go with the other duplicated components. Remember to drill a 5mm hole through the blank before turning.

9

Each wheel can now be finished, held on a small jam chuck.

10

The last turning job is to make the wheel-retaining pegs. African Blackwood is best for this, as it holds together in such small, detailed work. The pegs need to be about 10 mm ($3/8$") long with a knob on the head end and slightly tapered so they fit snugly in the tiny holes in each axle.

11

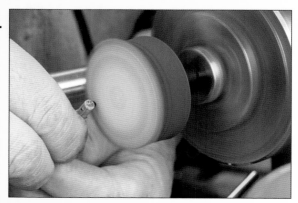

Once turned it is necessary to sand off the 'pip' on the top of each peg, a remainder from parting. This is most simply done once they are held in their respective holes.

12 For the final assembly I use cyanoacrylate (Superglue) and fine brass pins, but use what best suits you.

This truck is a suitable carriage for the three cannons that I make for Donay. The other two are The Cannon and Ball and The Cannon Ball and String. For this last puzzle a little modification is necessary... but that will be dealt with in my next book, with the complete instructions for The Cannon Ball and String.

Bibliography

The Principles and Practice of Ornamental or Complex Turning
by John Jacob Holtzapffel
Available through the Woodworker's Library®
(see Suppliers list p.117)

Hand or Simple Turning: Principles and Practice
by John Jacob Holtzapffel
Available through the Woodworker's Library®
(see Suppliers list p.117)

Bill Jones' Notes from the Turning Shop
by Bill Jones.
Now out of print

Bill Jones' Further Notes from the Turning Shop
by Bill Jones
Now out of print

Woodturning: A Foundation Course
by Keith Rowley
Available from the Woodworker's Library®
(see Suppliers list p. 117)

Woodturning Trickery
By David Springett

Suppliers

This list is by no means exhaustive, but may help a little.

Thread chasing tools

Craft Supplies USA
1287 East 1120 South
Provo, UT 84606
Phone 1-800-551-8876
www.craftsuppliesusa.com

Lathes and tools

Craft Supplies USA
1287 East 1120 South
Provo, UT 84606
Phone 1-800-551-8876
www.craftsuppliesusa.com

Woodcraft
PO Box 1686
Parkersburg, WV 26102
Phone 1-800-225-1153
www.woodcraft.com

Grizzly Industrial, Inc.
1821 Valencia St
Bellingham, WA 98229
Phone 1-800-523-4777
www.grizzly.com

Rockler Woodworking & Hardware
4365 Willow Dr
Medina, MN 55340
Phone 1-800-279-4441
www.rockler.com

Highland Hardware
1045 N. Highland Ave NE
Atlanta, GA 30306
Phone 1-800-241-6748
www.tools-for-woodworking.com

Woodworker's Supply
5604 Alameda Pl. NE
Albuquerque, NM 87113
Phone 1-800-645-9292
www.woodworker.com

Fine wood

MacBeath Hardwoods
930 Ashby Ave
Berkeley, CA 94710
Phone 1-800-479-9907
www.macbeath.com

Gilmer Wood Co.
2211 NW St. Helens Rd
Portland, OR 97210
Phone 1-888-667-3979
www.gilmerwood.com

Adhesives

Rockler Woodworking & Hardware
4365 Willow Dr
Medina, MN 55340
Phone 1-800-279-4441
www.rockler.com

Woodworker's Supply
5604 Alameda Pl. NE
Albuquerque, NM 87113
Phone 1-800-645-9292
www.woodworker.com

Books and videos

The Woodworker's Library®
2006 S. Mary
Fresno, CA 93721
Phone 1-800-345-4447
www.woodworkerslibrary.com

Woodcraft
PO Box 1686
Parkersburg, WV 26102
Phone 1-800-225-1153
www.woodcraft.com

Craft Supplies USA
1287 East 1120 South
Provo, UT 84606
Phone 1-800-551-8876
www.craftsuppliesusa.com

Highland Hardware
1045 N. Highland Ave NE
Atlanta, GA 30306
Phone 1-800-241-6748
www.tools-for-woodworking.com

Index

Books of related interest

A Treatise on Stairbuilding and Handrailing
by W & A Mowat.
The classic reprinted text for joiners, architects and fine craftsmen. Originally published in London in 1910. 390pp. Paper.

The Complete Manual of Wood Bending
by Lon Schleining.
Schleining provides instruction on each of three basic methods of producing curved work; laminate bending, steam bending, and milling. A complete course in bending. 190pp. Paper.

The Commercial Woods of Africa: A Descriptive Full Color Guide
by Peter Phongphaew.
Profiles 90 African Woods. A full set of relevant facts is provided for each tree, including a full-color photograph of each wood's grain and pattern. A list of botanical, commercial and vernacular names, a map indicating the tree's habitat in Africa, and descriptive text about the tree itself. 206pp. Hardcover.

Making Mantels
by David Getts
Over 200 color photographs in this book cover a broad range of mantel designs for the craftsman to consider. Plentiful examples of detailed plans guide the woodworker through the design, construction, and installation steps in mantel making. 192pp. Paper.

Woodcarving: Book 1 Basic Techniques
by Ian Norbury
17 quick and easy to carve projects for beginners. 86pp. Paper.

Sharpening With Waterstones: A Perfect Edge in 60 Seconds
by Ian Kirby.
Waterstones sharpen all your woodworking tools better, easier, and quicker than ever before. Master craftsman Ian Kirby teaches you a series of logical steps for putting a perfect edge on planes, knives, chisels, and carving tools. 112pp. Paper.

New Wood Puzzle Designs: A Guide to the Construction of Both New and Historic Puzzles
by James W. Follette.
Jim Follette offers 12 projects in four categories. Puzzles from cubes, puzzles from disks, puzzles from rings, and opening puzzles. Try "The Bolt to Drive you Nuts" or the "Hexagonal Dovetail Puzzle", you'll love them. 96pp. Paper.

Harvesting Urban Timber: A Complete Guide
by Sam Sherrill
Nearly three billion board feet of urban lumber is buried, chipped, burned or otherwise destroyed. Dr. Sherrill discusses how to alleviate some of this waste by harvesting the timber and using it for a variety of purposes. 186pp. Paper.

Making Working Wooden Locks
by Tim Detweiler
Complete plans for 5 working wooden locks. Amaze your friends. 96pp. Paper.

The Art of Segmented Woodturning
by Malcolm Tibbetts
A step-by-step guide to the art of combining various woods into turned objects. A complete guide to the subject. 184pp. Paper.

Building Cabinet Doors & Drawers
by Danny Proulx
A practical book that includes all styles and a thorough discussion of suitable joinery techniques. 112pp. Paper.

The Illustrated Guide to Cabinet Doors & Drawers: Design, Detail, and Construction
by David Getts
This is a must-have reference that covers the construction of all types of cabinet doors and drawers. Includes an extensive gallery of door and drawer styles, cabinet hardware, and what to use and how to install it. 186pp. Paper.